On Television

On Television

Stuart Hood and
Thalia Tabary-Peterssen

Pluto Press

First published 1997 by Pluto Press
345 Archway Road, London N6 5AA
and 22883 Quicksilver Drive, Sterling, VA 20166-2012, USA

www.plutobooks.com

British Library Cataloguing in Publication Data
A catalogue record for this book is available from the British
Library

Library of Congress Cataloging in Publication Data
Applied for

ISBN   0 7453 1110 5 hardback
ISBN   0 7453 1111 3 paperback

Printed on demand by Lightning Source

Contents

List of Abbreviations

BACC	Broadcast Advertising Clearance Centre
BARB	Broadcasters' Audience Research Board Ltd
BECTU	Broadcasting, Entertainment, Cinematograph and Theatre Union
BSB	British Satellite Broadcasting
BSC	Broadcasting Standards Commission
C5	Channel 5
CFPB	Campaign for Freedom in Press and Broadcasting
CLT	Compagnie Luxembourgeoise de Télédiffusion
CNN	Cable News Network
CTV	Channel Television
CWU	Communication Workers Union
DBS	direct broadcasting by satellite
DCTV	digital cable television
DSTV	digital satellite television
DTTV	digital terrestrial television
EEC	European Economic Community
ENG	electronic news gathering
FCC	Federal Communications Commission
FCG	Free Communications Group
IBA	Independent Broadcasting Authority
Intelstat	International Telecommunications Satellite Consortium
IPA	Institute of Practitioners in Advertising
IPPA	Independent Programmes Producers' Association
IPPR	Institute for Public Policy Research
IT	information technology
ITA	Independent Television Authority
ITC	Independent Television Commission
ITN	Independent Television News
ITV	Independent Television
LWT	London Weekend Television
MAI	Mills and Allen International
NHS	National Health Service

NTL	National Transmission Ltd
PPB	party political broadcasting
PSB	Public Service Broadcasting
quango	quasi-autonomous non-governmental organisation
RPI	retail price index
SES	Société Européenne des Satellites
TCI	Telecommunications International
TQR	total qualifying revenue
TW3	*That Was The Week That Was*
TWW	Television for Wales and the West
USO	universal service obligation
VCR	video-cassette recorder
VOD	video on demand
WARC	World Administrative Radio Conference

Introduction

The first edition of *On Television* appeared in 1980. In those days television was not thought of as an industry; the concept of public service was generally accepted; 'the consensus' held sway. This situation seemed likely to continue for some time. In contrast the present revised version of the book has been written at a moment of technological and organisational change in the television industry. The outcome of that change is unclear although certain trends are emerging. It is therefore inevitable that the authors should end up supplying more questions than answers.

Some things remain constant however – they concern the nature of the television medium, the role of ideology, the powers of the controlling bodies, the politics of broadcasting, the role of government.

The book discusses these matters in a way that the authors hope will prove useful to students in secondary and tertiary education who are beginning to study the media. They also hope that it may prove enlightening to members of the public who, however expert in finding their way round the schedules and cruising the channels, are often puzzled about who exactly provides the programmes and are not informed about the choices, commercial, industrial, ideological and political, that determine what they see on their screens.

The authors make no apology for considering these and other related matters from the Left of the political spectrum.

Acknowlegements

The authors wish to thank Andrew Goodman for a critical reading of the text to which he brought his acute intelligence and extensive knowledge.

1   Television – A Map of the Medium

In all except the most undeveloped and economically deprived communities, television is as easily available as water, gas or electricity. Just as we do not wonder where the water, the gas or the electricity come from, how they get to us, or what processes they go through, so we do not generally wonder how television pictures reach our homes. The images on our screens are experienced as the constant stream of a 'natural' phenomenon which, as with a tap, we can switch on or off at will. Or, as the head of the Federal Communications Commission which regulates television in the United States once famously said 'television is . . . a toaster with pictures' and we are not normally concerned with the workings of our toasters or the exact origins of our water when, for example, we run a bath. But in order to discuss the nature of television – as a medium of immense social importance and how that medium is controlled – it is useful to have some idea of the physical process of television broadcasting.

The Electromagnetic Spectrum

The transmission of television signals involves utilising certain portions of the electromagnetic spectrum. The spectrum is made up of the waves that pass through the atmosphere and through solids on earth, and which continually surround us. They include ultraviolet and infra-red rays (at opposite ends of the spectrum), the light waves that we experience as colours and the waves that can be used to carry a radio or television signal. The electromagnetic spectrum ranges from extremely short to extremely long waves but the range of frequencies available is finite and is thus a limited resource – a scarce public utility. National governments apportion space on their allotted part of the spectrum to different agencies. Apart from radio and television, space is given to emergency services like ambulances and fire services, to the police, to air traffic controls and to mobile phone users. Large parts of the spectrum are reserved for the military and for confidential and secret government communications.

Access to the spectrum for broadcasting purposes requires a licence from government. Pirate stations operate without a licence. In Britain the licensed broadcasters can be either non-profit-making (the BBC) or commercial (the Channel 3 companies, Channel 4 and Channel 5). But since they are given access to a scarce 'public utility' they are expected to provide a 'public service' in return for the privilege. This service is usually summed up as the requirement to inform, educate and entertain. Public service broadcasters have traditionally aimed to make the signal freely available to the maximum number of viewers or listeners. Increasingly, commercial interests deliver a signal encrypted – that is, transmitted in a coded form – which is available only on payment and viewable only with the aid of a decrypter on the receiver.

The size of the slice of spectrum needed for a broadcast signal (the channel) depends on the amount of information that must be conveyed. That in turn depends on the kind of signal that is being transmitted. Colour television, for instance, requires more band width than black and white. In the United Kingdom there are five terrestrial TV channels for BBC1, BBC2, ITV (Channel 3), Channel 4 and Channel 5.

Access to the spectrum has traditionally been controlled but free. At a time when the market is seen as the solution to most problems it is not surprising that the proposal has emerged that access to this public resource should be regulated by the purse – that users should pay for and establish property rights in the spectrum. No doubt this would delight the Treasury. The question is whether the public interest would be better served by market control of this area any more than other public resources or services that the market has taken over – water, gas, the health service.

The Television Signal – Analogue and Digital

In a television studio, television cameras scan the set by means of an electronic beam in a cathode-ray tube which responds to light levels. The camera transforms this light information into electronic signals. These signals are then either sent by cable to large television transmitters on the ground which pass them on to our home aerials (terrestrial television) or to a ground station which sends them into space to a satellite (satellite television). In the case of satellite television a ground station sends the electronic signals into space to a satellite orbiting the earth. The satellite reflects the signals back to earth where they may be received directly by a dish on our homes (direct broadcasting by satellite – DBS) or by a dish owned by a company which distributes the signal to subscribers by cable.

In our set the process is the reverse of the one in the studio. In our television sets, the electronic information coming from the transmitter or satellite is converted by means of a cathode tube into a stream of high-speed electrons. These are concentrated into a beam which appears on our screens as a spot of light. The beam, in synchronised movement with the scanning spot in the television camera, scans our screens causing the chemicals that coat them to glow. Our eyes perceive the result of this immensely rapid scanning process as complete images. The number of times the beam moves across the screen per second defines the 'lines standard'. The more often the screen is scanned the better and the sharper the picture. In Britain the lines standard is 625 lines per second, in France it is 825 lines, in the United States 525 lines. It is technically possible to broadcast and receive a picture which is scanned 1000 times a second; its adoption is a matter of cost. If and when this lines standard is adopted, television sets will have to be replaced.

Since the images on our screens are produced by the same process as those in the television cameras they are said to be analogues of each other. Early in the new century analogue television will have been replaced by digital television. In digital television, information from the cameras is turned into the 1/0, on/off 'bits' of binary mathematics which combine into 'bytes'. Bytes are the basic clumps of information used by all computers. All kinds of data – sound, pictures, print – can be digitalised and in that form stored, manipulated, combined and transmitted. This is a process which has already given us the high-quality digital sound recording of compact discs. When applied to television it has the advantage that the band width taken up on the spectrum is greatly reduced. In Britain the new frequency channels for digital television -- called multiplexes -- will be allocated to broadcasters to provide new services which will be either in the form of Digital Terrestrial Television (DTTV) or Digital Satellite Television (DSTV). DTTV will provide some thirty channels although there is some governmental lack of clarity over the projected date for the change-over of analogue to digital terrestrial broadcasting. The first digital satellite in Europe was launched in 1995 and DSTV began in Italy, Germany, the Netherlands and France in 1996. Murdoch's BSkyB is the only satellite television company broadcasting to the UK with DSTV technology in place, and Sky planned to begin DSTV in 1997. Sky has leased enough space on the digital satellites to allow for between 150 and 200 channels in the UK.

The Networks

When the television signal leaves the studio it is carried by cable to a transmitter from which it reaches our screens. In the case of terrestrial television, transmitters are set up at strategic points all over the country. Both the BBC and ITV depend on a large network of such transmitters. (Those serving ITV have been privatised and the 1996 Broadcast Bill agreed the sale of the BBC's transmitters.) The BBC aims at total coverage; the commercial network has always felt that there were parts of the country where the population was too thin on the ground to make the building of a special transmitter financially viable.

Television signals are subject to interference from high steel-framed buildings in towns and cities and from natural features like hills and mountains. If we are to receive a clear picture the nearest transmitter must be in line of sight and our aerial must point directly at it. If a locality is surrounded by hills it can be difficult to put down a signal and the place will lie in a kind of shadow. Either a special transmitter has to be built to lay down the signal (which can be expensive) or else the signal has to be taken to the individual sets by cable from some special receiver. This solution, which is a costly one, is only economically justifiable in highly populated districts. It was in such districts that the commercial rediffusion of the television signal by cable was first undertaken. Satellite transmissions do not suffer from the same handicaps because the signal can be beamed directly to a satellite dish wherever that may be located. It seems obvious that had the technology existed when television began, satellite broadcasting would have been a better solution than the building of networks of transmitters.

Satellite Television

Arthur C. Clarke, a visionary science fiction writer, published a famous paper on satellites in the magazine *Wireless World* while working in the RAF during the Second World War. Already the limitation of broadcasting by antenna due to the curvature of the earth had been realised by scientists and engineers. Clarke calculated that at 22,300 miles above the earth a satellite would take 24 hours for a complete orbit and that with three satellites spaced around the equator, the whole world could be linked in telecommunications. In 1964 Intelstat, the International Telecommunications Satellite Consortium, was formed in Washington. At that time it was assumed that only governments from the developed countries would be able to launch and maintain satellites. The Soviet government refused to join the consortium, developing Intersputnik, the satellite network whose members were limited to communist countries. By the end of the 1970s Intelstat had almost a hundred member countries and controlled fourteen satellites in various positions on what had been named the 'Clarke ring'. The Consortium channelled television, telephone calls and other data between 171 countries, carrying two-thirds of the world's international communications traffic and almost all international television transmissions. Intelstat's satellites were never intended for direct reception in homes, as they needed huge dishes located in remote areas.

In the beginning the satellite system was dominated by the USA. A large proportion of US military and diplomatic communications were carried by Intelstat. In the US the White House, during the Nixon administration, had pressed the Federal Communications Commission (FCC) to allow an 'open skies' policy for domestic communications satellites. As a result many privately-funded satellites were lodged on the Clarke Ring to provide a string of services from television to banking and mail-order. During the 1970s US influence decreased. Technological development reduced the size of receivers and by the mid-seventies five-metre dishes could pick up a good picture from the sky. Experiments in direct satellite broadcasting began in developed countries across the world, in Canada, Indonesia and Japan.

In January 1977 the International Telecommunications Union organised the World Administrative Radio Conference (WARC) with the purpose of sharing out the space on the Clarke Ring to individual nations. They were to divide the spectrum into broadcast frequencies which would be assigned to different countries. The physical space available on the Clarke Ring is finite. If two satellites use the same frequency they will interfere with each other, so there must be a distance of at least two degrees between each satellite. As satellites are powered by sunlight, most satellites are positioned a few degrees west of the country they are designed to serve to maximise the sun's power in the evening (prime broadcasting time), rather than early morning. (In theory satellites could provide a 24-hour service, but only with the back-up of huge and heavy batteries to power the night-time gap in solar energy.) The Clarke Ring was divided up into three regions: Region

One encompassed Europe, Africa, the USSR and Mongolia; Region Two covered all the Americas and Greenland, and Region Three contained Asia, Australia and the Pacific.

Today, satellites or 'birds' race around the Clarke Ring at 7000 miles an hour and at 22,300 miles above the earth's equator. This means that each satellite takes 24 hours to orbit the earth and as such appears stationary if observed from the ground (geostationary – *ge* as in *geography* being the Greek word for 'earth'). A satellite's average lifespan is approximately ten years during which time almost all the power it needs is drawn from the sun. Once a satellite is in position its solar panels are opened and angled towards the sun. These panels move as the satellite moves to catch the solar energy which allows the receivers to pick up signals from earth. Transponders amplify and transfer these signals to a higher frequency to avoid interference, and then bounce them back to earth. The area on earth that can receive these amplified signals from the satellites is called its 'footprint'. This 'footprint' often spills over national borders and can flout national laws, e.g. satellite hard-core porn programmes are illegal in Britain although these are bounced on to dishes in Britain transmitted by Dutch and Scandinavian networks. Closed political regimes are also challenged by the availability of programmes not produced under their control. Before the collapse of the Berlin Wall programmes received in East Germany from West German television representing the more attractive – and illusory – side of life in the capitalist West fuelled the growing discontent in the totalitarian communist block. In China satellite dishes are not officially allowed because the Chinese government perceives many foreign programmes to have unacceptable content.

Cable Television

The cable used for conveying television messages to the transmitters and television cable services to homes was for many years a coaxial copper cable, which is physically bulky and has a limited capacity. Coaxial cables are being replaced by fibre optic cables which are as fine as a human hair. Signals can be sent along them (at the speed of light) in the form of pulses generated by lasers. The capacity of optical cable is enormous – so great that an optical cable can carry a very large number of signals as well as having space to allow two-way communications thus making 'interactive' television possible. An old dream that receivers can also be transmitters is thus realisable.

Fibre optical cables have been installed by British Telecom in its main networks but not yet in local networks i.e. to homes, owing to cost. They are also used by cable companies for the distribution of telephone and television signals. The combination of fibre optic cable and a digitised signal will make it possible for a telephone line to carry a television picture. This technical development makes possible a convergence between telecommunications, broadcasting and computers. This convergence has, as we shall see, important implications for the structures and ownership of broadcasting.

2 The Flow of Images and Gatekeeping

Iconography

Whatever type of television reception a household has access to – whether from a terrestrial or a satellite station – the images they receive are juxtaposed in such a way as to recount a narrative which can be easily constructed by the target audience. In any given society, the citizens, (that is, the viewers), will have gone through a particular educational system and will have been conditioned by a multitude of influences – the press, the Church, peer-groups, families, political parties – to respond to certain key images which have been endowed with the power of symbols. In British society, for example, a red, white and blue flag may be expected to arouse feelings of patriotism; an alternative 'reading' of that image refers to it as 'the butcher's apron' because it is in some people's eyes the symbol for centuries of colonial repression. But for large numbers of British people it will bring up thoughts about 'our' country, and sensations of loyalty to the Crown. When the flag is shown on our screens the assumption in the mind of the broadcasters is that most people will accept these positive associations – that on this, as on many other 'readings', there is a consensus.

To see the importance of a quick succession – a montage – of images, take the short sequence at the beginning of the *News at Ten* on ITV. It begins with Big Ben and the Houses of Parliament and ends up with a close-up of the clock face followed by a close-up of the newsreader. The authority of Parliament is thus inextricably linked with ITN news and gives the impression of coming from the political nerve centre of our society. The accuracy of the nation's timepiece is synonymous, the image suggests, with the accuracy of the newscast. Each headline is read out in between the clock's chimes giving them the intonation of an oracle. The equating of ITN and the *News at Ten* with the institution of Parliament and with Big Ben powerfully suggests that these images are synonyms for power, authority and rightness. We are expected to decode them in terms which define and reinforce the dominant social structures in our society.

During the programme we see behind the newsreader row upon row of television monitors. This impressive array of hardware awes the viewer with a display of technological 'gear'; the multiplicity of images they carry suggests the multiplicity of sources available to the programme. Technological wizardry, sometimes accompanied by turning globes and world maps, implies that nothing that happens on the global, possibly the intergalactic newsfront, escapes ITN's omnipresent artificial eyes. Watched from the safety of our homes this inspired tension-building introduction arouses anticipation and a voyeuristic frisson at the images of chaos 'out there'. Like children being read ghoulish tales by a parent while tucked up in bed, we feel protected by the mediating newsreaders while they tell us of horrors in the real world.

Reading the Images

However, there is a problem about images: they are open to different and contradictory interpretations. How, for instance, should one read a shot of a man or woman in a camouflage uniform holding an automatic rifle? The broadcasters tell us how we should read the image. The text they put over the picture and their choice of language defines the persons we see on the screen as soldiers or freedom fighters, partisans or terrorists. The words are intended to anchor the required meaning. The choice of the 'right' text is an important editorial and political decision. We know from everyday experience that words can be used in an attempt to define us and ask us to go along with the ideology of the market. Thus we are described as 'customers' and no longer as 'passengers' when we travel by train. Health care has become the business of the 'health industry'. Broadcasting has become the 'broadcasting industry'. The words used to describe particular politicians and political groups indicate the judgements of the news organisations as to their standing. Thus, in the media, Saddam Hussein before the Gulf War, or Nicolae Ceausescu before the Romanian revolt, appeared as very different creatures from the monsters they were revealed to be in the 1990s. A change in the political situation, such as that in the 1990s in South Africa, can mean that the names applied to individuals and groups have to be changed as 'terrorists' become legitimately recognised politicians.

The words spoken to accompany the pictures on our screens are as carefully chosen and sifted as the images. There is a chain of 'gatekeepers', running from the reporter or correspondent who writes the first story to the editor who looks at the final script and alters a word here and there.

The Rules of Image-making

There are other important factors which govern the kind of pictures we see on our screens. The way people are framed, how 'tight' a shot is and from what angle, affect our visual relationship – our interpretation and response – to different people. Just as in our normal social intercourse we observe certain conventions about how close we come to other people and how close we allow them to come to us, so, when choosing their images, television cameras keep a certain distance from their subjects. There is around us all an imaginary space which we might define as the sphere of intimacy – 'kissing distance' – which only certain people in certain roles are normally allowed to penetrate. This space is generally respected by TV cameras. It is almost inconceivable that one should see on the television screen a large close-up of a figure of authority – say, a minister or international politician – particularly if it were to betray emotion, e.g. a close-up of Margaret Thatcher in tears as she left Downing Street for the last time.

Significantly, when cameras were allowed into Parliament, one of the rules laid down on coverage was that no 'off-the-record' reaction (or non-reaction) shots should be broadcast. The revealing cut-away to a Member of Parliament sleeping through the speech of one of their right honourable friends would therefore never reach our screens. Similarly, if an important person is being interviewed in the studio the director will not allow a camera to pick up signs of nervousness or impatience, for example, drumming fingers or a tapping foot. In the case of ordinary people, however, it is not unknown for the camera to come close in, particularly if the subject is in a state of uncontrolled emotional excitement, grief or joy. The camera frequently penetrates the intimacy sphere of women, implying a disregard for their privacy and a denial of their right to space, thereby sanctioning a disturbing voyeurism. Sportsmen and women too, although popular national figures, can be shown weeping as they win or lose an award for 'their country'.

The Politics of Images

You will search in vain in the handbooks or 'grammars' of film and television for a discussion of the way subjects should be shot. In manuals dealing with camera technique and direction the framing of shots and the juxtaposition of images is certainly discussed, but always in terms of aesthetics and visual 'common sense'. What is not generally acknowledged or discussed is that an aesthetic judgement can conceal or embody a political one and that images chosen on the basis of decisions which are 'natural' or 'common sense' will certainly not be images that challenge the dominant ideology.

Thus a cameraman filming a monument to the victims of Bloody Sunday in Derry was observed to frame the shot in such a way as to avoid the 'unaesthetic' gap on either side of the memorial. Tight framing did, it is true, cut out distracting activity from passers-by, but it also eliminated an inscription below the official one, an inscription added by the IRA to commemorate the 'victims of British imperialism'.

Actuality and ENG

Those images which are selected to appear on our television screens are obviously only a tiny sample of the infinite choice offered by the world around us. The ones chosen fall into two categories: those which reflect what is called 'actuality', that is to say, events which are happening as we see them on our sets (or which happened fairly recently); and those which belong to the realm of fiction, such as the actions in a play, sitcom or film. Those in the first category are sometimes seen as being what marks television off from all the other representational arts, such as film, painting or photography, in that the pictures offered by television are 'live'. Through them we see events as they occur.

In the last 25 years or so the coverage has been revolutionised by the development of electronic news-gathering (ENG). News-gathering was once dependent on film, which had to be shot, developed and brought back to the news studio. This could cause a delay of many hours or days in the case of stories from other continents.

Today, portable electronic cameras are in use and the material they provide is sent back by satellite either for live transmission or recording, thus overcoming geographical distance. This also allows television organisations to circumvent problems with political regimes where independent television and freedom of the press are unknown or severely limited. Thus the peaceful student demonstrations and subsequent massacre in Tiananmen Square on the night of 3–4 June 1989 were broadcast to the world in 'real time'. The most striking recent example of how live coverage becomes more real than reality was provided by

CNN (Cable News Network), the American news channel, during the Gulf War. CNN reporters in Iraq used an independently powered, portable four-line telephone system to send a 'feed' from the roof of their hotel to a satellite truck positioned across the frontier in Jordan. From the truck the signal was bounced off a satellite and into CNN's station headquarters in Atlanta. Bush, Gorbachev and Saddam Hussein himself are all known to have watched CNN news coverage during the Gulf War making CNN at that moment the most influential television news agency in the world. While CNN continued to cover the war as closely as possible, other television organisations allowed themselves to be restricted to material provided by the US Army and its spokesmen. Much of it consisted of images that turned the deployment of the destructive weaponry of modern war into a kind of video game.

Gatekeeping

The process of choosing certain pictures and names and rejecting others is an example of what is often described as 'gatekeeping'. This figure of speech is taken from the way in which a farmer stands at the door of a pen and, by moving a gate from side to side as the cattle or sheep pass through, separates them out for dipping, for the market or the slaughterhouse. Gatekeeping is an essential function of any editor. Those who are employed as news-gatherers need to understand the requirements of the gatekeepers if they want their work to get on air. These requirements are either made explicit in policy documents or absorbed from colleagues, for example, in the canteen or at meetings where programmes are reviewed. Conformity with such official and unofficial guidelines is a prerequisite for promotion or continued employment. These rules are internalised by broadcasting professionals, most of whom are unconscious of the degree to which their judgements are shaped by them. They are not involved in some conspiracy of misinformation but acting in accordance with criteria which they describe as 'natural' or 'common sense'.

There are some events for which coverage cannot be provided and a convention has been established to deal with them. For example, a Cabinet meeting is by definition not open to the media. What television falls back on are shots of the coming and goings of ministers while a political correspondent provides a voice-over commentary on the importance of the occasion. Such pictures are little more than moving wallpaper – routine images on which the editors of television newscasts depend.

In the case of outside broadcasts, whether satellite or terrestrial, gatekeeping takes place as the events unroll; but the very fact that the broadcast is taking place is the result of gatekeeping at another level, in the shape of the editorial decision to commit resources such as cameras and outside broadcast vans to cover that particular event rather than some other of more or less equal interest and importance. The words 'interest' and 'importance' – 'important' to whom? 'interesting' to whom? – seem on the face of it simple but in reality they conceal a number of complicated assumptions about the audience and its interests and the role of television in society.

A freelance news reporter who has professional equipment necessary to provide news coverage for television stations looks around for a story. The first decision is whether a story is worth covering at all. In making this decision the reporters will probably look for some factor that distinguishes the situation from the normal run. If the story is about political asylum seekers, are there some other factors – political, personal, dramatic, emotional – that would lead it to be considered somehow different, exceptional, important and defined as 'news'? Once on to an incident the news crew may then go off to shoot some footage of the situation, probably after clearing with television newsroom staff that they are interested in the story. On arriving at the scene they will, once again, decide what aspects of the event make the most 'interesting' and/or acceptable report, and therefore what footage to collect.

Crucial Choices

How the process of gatekeeping informs the attitude of television journalists in their choice of material, including the images caught by the cameras, was revealed by a BBC cameraman covering the Basra Road massacre during the Gulf War. Interviewed after the war he said that he 'filmed it as I would any news event really, I . . . didn't actually show the horror of it, because I . . . produce material suitable for transmission, rather than, perhaps, reflecting what was actually there'.

This meant that he avoided filming the true extent of the carnage, but took 'the odd shot from the back, and the side which alluded to the fact that there were dead people there'. However a woman colleague, also interviewed after the war, shot images that she knew 'were unacceptable images for British television', because she wanted to show the horror of what she felt was an 'unacceptable event'. This consciously uncensored material she also knew to be 'not immediately usable in news terms' because of the censorship involved in the gatekeeping or editing processes that decide what are 'acceptable images' for British television.

Technological developments which provide a live unbroken reportage are still subject to gatekeeping. This ranges from what the camerapeople on the spot choose to film, to where the commentators are arranged in the studio, what their commentary consists of, and when the images cut from them to the 'live' action. All these decisions have a huge effect on how a narrative is constructed and received and what value judgements are incorporated into that narrative. The view of the directors of outside broadcasts and of their professional commentators is that the only narrative that concerns them is what happens in terms of the progress of the game or sporting event. But what if events are taking place on the margin of the event which merit being covered and commented on? They are, in practice, ignored. It required the attack by Arab terrorists on Israeli athletes at the 1972 Olympic Games to draw the attention of the cameras away from the athletic events. Sports commentators who command an enormous audience and who therefore have considerable potential influence, have chosen to ignore incidents where black and Asian players are subject to racial abuse. They, and the cameras, do not see the incidents just as they apparently do not see the occasional 'streaker'. Whatever has 'nothing to do with the game', however socially revealing it may be, does not get aired.

A New Use of the Term

The concept of the gatekeeper has taken on a new meaning: the delivery of programmes by cable and satellite and the use of encrypted signals which can only be unscrambled if the viewer pays for a special decrypting gadget or subscribes to certain channels on a cable service. Clearly if any company had a monopoly over the means of decrypting television signals that company would come to control a 'gateway'. A whole range of programmes would cease to be available to viewers who did not have or could not afford a decrypter. Whoever controls access to satellite channels capable of carrying digital television and establishes a monopoly over the rights in decrypters will be a powerful gatekeeper with a vast amount of control over global information and culture.

Setting the Agenda

Closely connected with the process of gatekeeping is the function known as 'agenda-setting'. This is a term used to describe the way in which those who work in the medium of television define the context within which a topic is discussed on the air and in front of the cameras. The process can typically begin offscreen when the producer responsible for a programme like *Newsnight* or *Panorama* discusses with the interviewer what questions should be put to the interviewee, whether that person is a politician, a trade unionist, a celebrity of some kind, or a member of the public who has suddenly and briefly become 'news'. Between them they will decide what ground should be covered in the interview and will go over the main questions to be put during the broadcast.

On one level this is a sensible and practical step to prevent the discussion from wandering or running out of time. (Both considerations, of course, contain unspoken assumptions about the attention span of the audience and the nature of human discourse.) But it can also be a way of refusing to discuss certain aspects of a topic and of steering the discussion away from difficult areas. A similar conversation may take place with the interviewee, particularly if he or she is politically important. 'We thought we ought to cover the following points', the interviewer may typically say, the incorporation of the interviewee in the 'we' being an important trick of language and one that makes it more difficult for the interviewee to refuse to agree with the proposal. It is, of course, always open to the interviewee at this point to suggest other areas for discussion; but unless he or she is very persuasive or very powerful (in the sense of possessing social or political weight), it is unlikely that the interviewer will accept the counterproposals.

Free Discussion?

Another form of agenda-setting is to be found in so-called 'programmes of debate', such as *Question Time*. The choice of guests, the choice of questions, the choice of shots and the mediation of the presenter all effectively control the context and the texts of the debates. Unwelcome or obstreperous members of the studio audience are unlikely to be shown on screen, and their voices will literally be silenced by the choice the director makes of who is offered and who is denied the microphone. The presenter can be observed on screen to cut off a speaker or to allow a speaker time; the director has the offscreen power to decide what camera to use, what shot and what sound. Control of the situation is often facilitated by the geography of the studio, or the way in which sets are constructed which determines the physical distance between presenter, a panel of guest speakers and the audience drawn from 'the public'. In many cases the audience face the 'panel of experts', or are too far from each other to allow normal conversational exchanges and the possible breaking of television conventions. Even when these arrangements are not adopted and presenters move among the studio audiences with their portable microphones in their hands they can still exercise a large measure of control over the participants.

However, a new kind of discussion programme is now firmly established where tension is built in and encouraged. Obvious examples are *The Oprah Winfrey Show* and Esther Ranzten's adversarial programmes. Naturally, there is still highly sophisticated control of the proceedings by the presenter. It is noticeable that such shows deal with interpersonal matters involving 'ordinary people' and not with politicians or members of other socially priviliged groups.

Alternative Tactics

Agenda-setting is of more than academic interest – it is also something which one can learn to observe while watching television interviews. By studying the way agenda-setting works members of the public who are likely to find themselves in front of a television camera can develop counterstrategies. Many politicians have developed such techniques; a common one is to say: 'Before answering that question (that interesting question) may I just say . . . ' They then proceed to make the one point which they intended to put across when they agreed to be interviewed. It is not for nothing that the main political parties and important interest groups within society give their members training in interviewing techniques in television studios where they acquire the skills of the game. Members of political or interest groups which lie outside the parliamentary or ideological consensus are not likely to have the same training facilities or to be treated with the same consideration. The rules of interviewing are in that sense unfair. Some organisations on the Left respond to the unequal rules by refusing to appear at all on television unless they have complete control of the situation.

Direct Access

Complete control is possible only in two circumstances: one of these is a general election political party broadcast. These are arranged between the parliamentary parties and the broadcasters, that is, the BBC and the ITC. The parties have complete editorial control. A party qualifies only if it puts fifty or more candidates in the field at a General Election. In the case of a small party the cost of putting up fifty or more deposits in order to have air-time makes the resulting broadcast an exceedingly expensive commercial. The other possible opportunity for complete editorial control is an access programme, like *The Slot* on Channel 4, where 'viewers present their opinions on issues of the day' even if only for ten minutes a week, or *Link*, a 15-minutes-long programme on ITV 'made by disabled people primarily for disabled people'.

One of the original access programmes was the BBC's *Open Door*, which on one occasion allowed a Southall group to express their views on police brutality during the anti-National Front demonstration in which Blair Peach was killed. Recently there has been an increase in the 'video diary' programme format. Members of the public are given video cameras with which to record their own narratives. The BBC's *Video Nation* is a long-running example. But it must be remembered that editorial choices are still being made as to who is to broadcast and on what subject. On top of these selections, final editorial control of any individual's footage will always lie with the producers of such programmes and ultimately with the governors of each television institution who are, in law, the broadcasters or publishers. In the final analysis they are responsible for everything that goes out in their name and are therefore wary of being involved in legal actions over libel or other breaches of the law.

The Dominant Ideology

Every television institution is hierarchical, and as such, those at the top of the pyramid will tend by the very nature of their position and power to identify with establishment ethics and the maintenance of a system. They have internalised its mores, codes and regulations. They will promote the dominant ideology of capitalism and the patriarchy.

Who is it that applies these judgements in practice? The answer is the executives and programme makers in the BBC and the television companies who are by social origin predominantly but not exclusively middle-class. If of working-class origins they will in all probability have been assimilated into the middle class in the course of their education, which will normally include not only full-time education up to the age of 17 or 18 but also further education at college or university. At one time there were among those recruited to the BBC a number of bright young men from Oxbridge – the so-called 'high flyers' – who were thought of as potential senior executives or even as director generals. Today the net is cast more widely, and a 'minority tap system', which picks off graduates with first-class degrees from other universities, is implemented.

The broad but undeniably clear picture is that they will be for the most part white, male and middle-class, and that they will normally and predominantly espouse the ideology of the dominant social structures. Their decisions will reflect and reinforce that ideology. Even if the unimaginable happened and a licence to broadcast were awarded to a group whose politics and philosophies challenged the status quo there would still be the problem of funding. Television production is an extremely costly business – the 1996 BBC drama serialising the life of Cecil Rhodes, for example, had a budget of £10 million – making it unlikely that any group challenging patriarchal or capitalist ideology would be in a financial position to license and run its own television station. The only possibility left to groups who oppose elements of the dominant ideology is to make videos with the now-available cheaper equipment for localised distribution and viewing on video recorders, which are readily accessible. This is a tactic that is used in business and will be increasingly adopted by those who find their access to the medium blocked politically.

3 The Audience

Camcorders are now commonplace and people are becoming used to being filmed on tape. Indeed some events, like weddings, are increasingly edited at post-production, giving people outside the film and broadcast industry an idea of how images are manipulated and constructed from – sometimes very different – raw footage. But such moments apart, most people are still unlikely ever to find themselves in front of professional film or television cameras in a studio or elsewhere, although the chances of being recorded by security or police video equipment are now high. We will remain anonymous 'members of the audience' for television, of 'the public' – two terms which are sometimes used on television as if they were the same thing. The concept of 'the audience' is obviously important for the television professionals, as it is indeed for anyone who is engaged in the business of communication. In the case of television, it is particularly important because of the unquantifiable and invisible nature of the television audience. Lecturers or politicians at a public meeting can see and gauge the size of their audiences; a newspaper editor has a return of sales which gives a measurable approximation of the size of the readership; but the television professional often has a desperate feeling that the programme just broadcast, on which a great deal of time and energy has been spent, may have been both unseen and unheard.

Counting Heads

However, audiences can be measured. Nowadays both the BBC and the ITV use the same method to quantify their viewers. BARB (Broadcasters' Audience Research Board Ltd) is a joint company set up by the BBC and the Independent Television Association, the collective association representing the commercial television companies. Its board of directors also has directors representing the IPA (Institute of Practitioners in Advertising), Channel 4 , Channel 5 and BSkyB (representing satellite broadcasters). Its job is to provide information on audiences for the whole of the television industry, for broadcasters, advertising agencies and advertisers.

To compute audience size, BARB uses a statistical method known as sampling which is well-tried and familiar from opinion polls. A number of receivers are provided with a device which shows what programmes were watched and for how long. This includes programmes recorded by the set-owners and viewed within seven days in what is called 'time-shift-viewing'. The 'sample' consists of a relatively small number of sets – about 4500 in all, whose owners are representative of the social and economic mix of viewers as a whole. (The panel members get a nominal incentive payment.) The information from the meters is retrieved automatically overnight by a computer. From that information it is possible to extrapolate reliable statements about the size of the total audience.

The Ratings

The viewing figures thus arrived at are the ratings. They are used to assess the commercial viability and popularity of a programme in particular and of a television channel in general.

In the case of commercial television this assessment is vitally important to the advertisers. Commercial television has been cynically defined as a way of delivering an audience to an advertiser, the programmes being the bait to attract the audience to watch the advertisements that go out in the commercial breaks. The advertiser judges the usefulness of advertising on television by how much it costs to buy the attention of each 1000 viewers; this figure is called the 'cost per thousand'. This traditional calculation provides a strong incentive for commercial television companies to obtain the largest possible audiences and thus maximise their profits. The cost per thousand differs from region to region, the most expensive being London and the South-East where the much more competitive advertising market drives prices up. To advertise to a thousand people for thirty seconds, LWT, (London Weekend Television) currently charges an average of £7.15 while Border is the cheapest at £2.53.

However, advertisers are not satisfied with mere numbers. The audience delivered to them must be of the right kind, have the right demographics, that is, be composed of the kind of person who has the purchasing power to buy the products advertised. Thus the demographics of ITV's The *South Bank Show* were described as good, 45 per cent of its viewers being in the ABC1 socio-economic groups (those with most disposable income) and 25 per cent of them aged 16–34. What the advertisers look forward to are technological innovations which will develop interactive shopping and allow the advertisers to build profiles of individual viewers.

As far as an advertiser is concerned, to broadcast a commercial for an expensive car to an audience made up of a large number of women (who are traditionally unlikely to make the decision to buy the car) or of pensioners or children (who have not the purchasing power to buy one) is a waste of money. What they want is an audience of men in the top socio-economic groups which are defined in terms of spending power. Indeed, ITV has in recent times been criticised by advertisers as appealing to an audience that contains too many older people and too many members of the working class – people with little available cash.

The desire to target audiences more precisely has led to the concept of 'niche' audiences which might, for example, be a predominantly male audience (potential car-buyers) attracted to sports programmes or else what has been described as a 'Sunday colour supplement audience' with specific cultural interests and money in their pockets. A further development is the narrowing-down of the 'niche' in what is called 'particle advertising'. This is being explored in conjunction with digital television and the possibility of viewer/customer interaction with material shown on the screen. It is advertising targeted at the individual viewer and his or her tastes and interests.

The BBC and the Ratings

Ratings are also important for the BBC. This may sound surprising since as a public service organisation it has, so far, no commercial reason to maximise audiences. But the size of the BBC's audience is politically important; the BBC depends for its income on the licence fee paid by owners of television sets. The licence is like a gun licence or a car licence; it gives the owner the right to operate the set. It is what is called a regressive tax because the fee is the same for all set-owners regardless of their income. The size of the licence fee is determined by the government. By a longstanding convention the government passes on the money collected from the licence fees – in 1995 it came to £1.8 billion – to the BBC. It has been established in the courts that you cannot refuse to pay the licence on the grounds that you never watch the BBC.

The licence is unpopular with the public and with the politicians who represent them. This unpopularity has led some politicians to put pressure on the BBC to move towards subscription television as an alternative method of financing its operations. Were the BBC unable to demonstrate that it has a reasonable share of the audience it would become politically vulnerable. Low ratings would make it difficult for the BBC to ask for an increase in the licence fee, to deal with, for instance, rising operating costs. Worse still, politicians might begin to ask why people should pay a tax to support an institution whose programmes they do not wish to watch. The BBC therefore aims to establish over its two channels, BBC1 and BBC2, an audience share that is roughly comparable to that obtained by the two commercial channels, ITV and Channel 4.

Using the Ratings

Ratings have an obvious part to play in programme planning and the deployment of resources. Questions are asked in making programming decisions: if the audience is (in television terms) very small, how can the employment on programme X of expensive capital equipment and highly paid staff be justified? What is the smallest audience that a television organisation can afford (in terms the accountants will understand) to address? Ratings can also be used to confirm programme judgements. Thus if a programme designed to be popular gets a low audience, that programme requires re-evaluation; on the other hand, if what was thought of as a minority programme gets good ratings, this is also significant for future programming decisions.

The Mass Audience

A naive reading of ratings might regard the very large audiences they sometimes register – the 21 million who tuned to the interview of Princess Diana on *Panorama*, for instance – as a homogenous whole. But research demonstrates that appreciation of a programme varies widely. BARB has set up a panel of 3000 adults who rate each programme they watch on a scale from 0 to 10. This produces an Appreciation Index which unlike the ratings is confidential. It is, says BARB, 'a valuable tool . . . in the planning of future schedules'.

In fact viewers' reactions can range from acceptance to indifference, from incomprehension to rejection. Inertia too plays a part. Some of the audience may continue to watch a programme simply as part of the evening's unbroken flow of moving images and because there is no more attractive alternative. Those who reject the programme, on the other hand, may continue to watch precisely because they dislike what they see and wish to react to it with critical comments, disrespect for the speakers and so on. The diversity of the audience and the variety of its reactions to programmes is extremely important when it comes to discussing the social and political effects of television.

How is the Audience Defined?

How is the audience defined in the minds of the broadcasters? The view of the audience as predominantly nuclear family units is still reflected in much of what we see on the screen. In commercials, the housewife is still ensuring the continued happiness of her family by buying Brand X washing powder, or Brand Y cereal. Current affairs programmes are still addressed specifically to 'those of you sitting at home'. Social and political questions are presented in terms of the family and of its budget, as if the only interests of the individual members of that family were those defined in terms of home, the hearth or the television set. Occasionally viewers are assumed to have special 'minority' interests such as gardening or cookery but the activities discussed tend to be domestic and household-orientated.

Life outside the family is generally portrayed by young adults in sexual terms, from comedy programmes like *Men Behaving Badly* to commercials for aftershave, cars and deodorants. Men − and particularly women − represented on television with interests other than these, as political citizens with problems and social aims outside the domestic circle or sexual circuit are few and far between.

The way in which the members of the television audience is defined reinforces that process of socialisation in family groups which many forces in our society are happy to perpetuate. How much of these stereotypical representations is responsible for the fact that the man within the real family unit is still the one who holds the remote control, and who has first choice of the programmes to be watched on a shared TV set?

Audience Awareness

As we saw in Chapter 2 the images on the television screen are never haphazard. They aim to convey a message whether in the form of news, sport, drama, or advertising. It is assumed by the image-makers that the members of the audience will accept the 'preferred reading'. This is one of the ways in which television can, with varying success, attempt to mould opinion among the audience. The 'preferred reading' embodies a common-sense view of world events and situations. It is the reading of 'reasonable' people.

Thus during the Gulf War the news coverage eschewed antiwar images or text, and those involved were portrayed positively, some as heroes. In periods of industrial disputes television audiences are frequently told that 'the public' or 'the customers/consumers' are fed up with strikes, that 'the public' would not stand for much more, that 'the public' resents strikers in public services. Sometimes the concept of 'the public' is extended to include the programme presenters who in interviews would use phrases like 'we, as members of the public'. The presenters, the viewers and 'the public' are projected as a body that share the same thoughts and feelings, although, of course, many of 'the public' would be the very people on strike.

Any member of the public who is likely to appear live on television must be prepared to counter-attack. When very highly paid interviewers suggest that 'we, the members of the public' are fed up with the demands from low-paid workers for a wage rise, they should be asked what their take-home pay is; if asked 'You are a trade unionist, doesn't this mean that you are politically motivated?' the interviewee should enquire whether the interviewer is a trade union member and what his or her motives are. It has to be said that this takes considerable courage because the atmosphere of the studio is intimidating and we have been conditioned into thinking that we must 'behave' when on camera. Members of groups likely to be interviewed should study the media, practise interviewing techniques and get in touch with people in the media who have the knowledge and willingness to help. Already Small World, a London-based company, has been established to train minority groups experiencing police persecution and unjust legal charges during civil conflict to record their own videos as documentary evidence as happened in the anti-poll tax demonstrations in 1989/90.

Stereotypes and Shared Values

Communication of any kind could naturally not take place unless there were some shared views common to the audience and the communicators. What has to be considered in the case of television is the extent to which it contributes towards shaping these views. In comedy shows, for instance, it is assumed that certain situations will be experienced as funny by a large portion of the audience; their views on a wide variety of questions, from the relationships between the sexes to class and racial relations, are taken for granted and the jokes are made to fit these assumptions.

In this process stereotypes play an important part. There are racial stereotypes – Irish, Scots, Cockneys, Afro-Caribbeans are common examples – but so are rapacious parasitic women: the sister-in-law in *Frasier*, butt of many jokes, who never gets to appear on screen, the next-door neighbour in *Birds of a Feather* and of course Patsy in *Absolutely Fabulous*. Cantankerous old people also abound on the 1990s screen, as do sexist and homophobic attitudes evident in the highly popular but reactionary *Have I Got News For You*.

'Only Entertainment'

The view that comedy shows cannot be dismissed as 'only entertainment', and that to invite audiences to laugh at certain jokes is to ask them to collude in sexism and racism, invokes the charge of being a tiresome, humourless, niggling espouser of political correctness (itself an easy and common target for ridicule). It all depends, the argument runs, on the context in which the character is portrayed and the jokes made. Jo Brand, for example, making 'sizeist' jokes about herself is parodying the sexist and sizeist jokes made by many male comedians. Basil Fawlty is clearly a pompous bigot, a parody of the xenophobic, provincial British businessman and the jokes are on him, rather than about the archetypal nagging wife or the incompetent pet-monkey waiter whose every mistake is explained by his being 'from Barcelona'. When *Fawlty Towers* was bought by Spanish television, Manuel's nationality changed to Portuguese. Each society has its own stereotypes. Sexist or racist views are not necessarily shared by the writers or actors in these shows. They may well believe that they are holding certain social attitudes up to ridicule, that they are being ironic. But irony does not travel well, and not all the audience reaction will be what the authors intended. Moreover a racist or sexist joke is no less racist or sexist for being funny or even witty. To criticise comedy, whether in the form of a verbal joke, or a situation comedy, is not to deny its place in pleasurable human communication or to overlook the fact that comedy is probably always unfair.

The Cult of Nostalgia

In television drama one of the most marked trends in the 1990s has been towards nostalgia: for the Edwardian era (the 1995 adaptation of Edith Wharton's *The Buccaneers*), for the First World War (the adaptation of Catherine Cookson's *The Cinder Path*), for the Second World War (the recent adaptation of Mary Wesley's *The Camomile Lawn*), for the 1960s (the series *Heartbeat*) and for the Regency period in the highly successful and popular adaptation of Jane Austen's *Pride and Prejudice*. This is a phenomenon of considerable interest and importance which is characterised by the interpretation of history in terms of personal and usually romantic relationships and of aesthetics and is the essence of costume drama as presented on television.

The televising of nostalgia plays on the audience's insecurities and invites them to share in the escapism which is inherent in a romantic turn to the past. To accept this reading of history is to accept a specific way of looking at society and human relationships within it. In this case too we may speak of preferred readings which are reinforced by the authority of broadcasting institutions which produce them with professional skill.

The trend towards nostalgia is not confined to television – witness the commemorations and celebrations of the fiftieth anniversary of the Second World War, but it is difficult today to separate a public event from a media one, especially if it promotes a sense of national importance. The habit of looking back is caused by deep unease about the future, and is a reflection of, on the one hand, the general economic and political crisis of capitalism and, on the other, of the ecological disasters that threaten the planet.

Another increasingly noticeable programme trend focuses on the supernatural. What purport to be factual programmes as well as fictional ones dealing with aspects of the supernatural feature prominently in the schedules of both the BBC and the commercial companies. Broadcasting 'evidence' of spiritual phenomena exploits the audience's desire for 'information' that suggests a meaning beyond chaotic human existence, a need which is symptomatic of the Zeitgeist at the end of the millennium.

The Interactive Audience

Until the end of the twentieth century the role of the viewer has been essentially passive. Notice of our views has only been taken indirectly through the ratings, and minimally from the 'why-oh-why' letters aired for a chummy ten minutes on *Points of View*. More recently a small number of Channel 4 community programmes such as *Right to Reply* brought the viewers on to the screen to air their opinions about television output.

Today, backers of digital television spend a lot of time promoting the idea of 'interactive' television. David Elstein, when at BSkyB, presented digital television as being an opportunity for the viewer to gain 'freedom from the scheduler' and thus to exercise more control over their choice of programmes. Other much vaunted interactive services to become available will include home banking and home shopping, and the idea of home voting has been proposed. So-called interactive viewers' response here will be limited to a decision whether to part instantly with their money or not, and whether to do business with banks from home. This interaction is purely to facilitate the movement of money.

Apart from the novelty of these 'interactive' services, representatives of the companies pioneering digital television have enthused about viewer participation in 'interactive' programmes. On the face of it this would seem to usher in a new age when the role of the viewer will become pro-active, and the possibility of shaping our broadcast future will be offered. Already programmes debating current issues have included the viewer by phone, giving a series of telephone numbers which the viewers can ring to register their vote for or against a motion. Some pundits suggest that on digital television, viewers will be able to build a programme from a choice of alterative plots and characters, similar to the developments in CD-Rom games. This proposed freedom has a fundamental flaw. It is a freedom offered to the viewer with the money to buy the new technology, the money to subscribe to the services which offer 'interaction'. The concept of viewers' universal access will change. Core services may well still be offered in exchange for the licence fee, but 'interaction' will not be universally available. It is possible that future public debates will take place on interactive television, but the audience and participators will be part of an audience elite, and an underclass will emerge whose viewing is limited and whose voice is not heard.

4   The History of Terrestrial Television

Since the beginning of terrestrial television in Britain in 1936, fundamental social changes have occurred in British society. The austerity of the war years and their immediate aftermath, with which the 1945 Labour government had to struggle, was followed by the economic boom of the 1950s. This was the period when the Conservative government claimed that we had 'never had it so good'. There followed a period of economic crisis for which successive Labour governments could offer no solutions. When Margaret Thatcher came to power in 1979, British capitalism enthusiastically adopted the policies she advocated. Fundamental to these policies was the view that the market must be given free play in all spheres. Trade unions had to be deprived of their rights in order to allow employers to depress wages. In the health service, a market was set up in which doctors and hospitals competed for patients. In education, a business ethic replaced the concept of education as something more than an intellectual discipline or a vocational training. In broadcasting, an internal market was introduced. Accountants and business consultants moved in and applied the inappropriate criteria of industrial production to cultural production.

The Thatcher years have left their mark on how we are expected to think of our roles in society. As always, language is the bearer of ideology. We are no longer 'passengers' who are offered a service, but 'customers' who are buying one. Broadcasting, in its turn, is no longer a public service but an industry: the BBC is 'sold' as both a product and a brand name by its own screen advertising, and viewers have become consumers.

It is important not to believe that these policies were the invention of Margaret Thatcher alone. Thatcherism was a response to the needs and pressures of important economic and political forces which believed that if Britain was to be competitive and economically successful in the world market, it must be ruthless at home. As a Conservative minister famously remarked, a certain amount of unemployment was a price worth paying for a competitive edge.

The Cosy Duopoly – BBC and ITV

The history of terrestrial television in Britain falls into two distinct periods. The first is one in which the BBC had a monopoly. This lasted from 1936 to 1955 with an interruption during the Second World War. In 1955 the monopoly was broken by the introduction of commercial television – Independent Television (ITV). For almost forty years the two systems existed unchallenged, competing for audiences – which they came to divide fairly equally between them – and becoming partners in what has been described as a 'cosy duopoly'. That duopoly survived the arrival of BBC2 in 1964, but was challenged by the advent of Channel 4 in 1982. The fight for the audience was now a three-cornered one. The arrival of Channel 5 in 1997 fragmented the audience still further. More crucially, terrestrial television is having to face the prospect of increasing competition from cable and satellite broadcasting. It is a far cry from the days when the BBC inaugurated what is acclaimed as the world's first regular public television service.

BBC Television – The Public Service Remit

This service was started by the BBC at Alexandra Palace in north London on 2 November 1936. It was almost exactly ten years since the British Broadcasting Company, set up by radio manufacturers shortly after the 1914–18 war to transmit programmes of speech and music and thus encourage sales of sets, had been transformed into the British Broadcasting Corporation – a non-profit-making monopoly. It is ironic in the light of more recent Tory policies that it was a Conservative government that in 1927 backed the change from the BBC as a commercial company to the BBC as a public corporation set up under a Royal Charter and financed by the licence which each owner of a radio set was required to pay. The Charter spelt out that the BBC should be a non-profit-making organisation and that it had a duty to 'inform, educate and entertain'.

The governors appointed as the Corporation's first director general and chief executive John Reith, a formidable puritanical figure, who had been general manager of the British Broadcasting Company. He was to set his stamp on the BBC and establish the Reithean tradition of public service broadcasting.

Even before the Second World War (1939–45) the BBC had built up a reputation in radio as a national institution. Its importance as a source of information and as an instrument of social cohesion was immense, as was its prestige as the 'voice of the nation'. In 1936 a government committee on broadcasting recommended that a television service should be undertaken by the BBC 'as an adjunct to their [radio] broadcasting service'.

Before the Second World War a television set was an expensive novelty few could afford. Coverage was confined to London and the Home Counties. The programmes offered were largely based on the middle-class concept of a night out in the West End. The single most prestigious (and it must be said) pioneering programme was the outside broadcast covering the coronation of George VI in 1938. When war was declared against Germany in September 1939, television transmission was closed down, the fear being that the one and only transmitter at Alexandra Palace might be used by German bombers as a radio beacon. Television was not to come on air again until 1946.

The Post-war Monopoly

In the ten years immediately following the Second World War the content of television programming was still genteel and bland. High principles and prestige had degenerated into stuffiness and complacency. In this atmosphere the new and growing medium of television faced difficulties, particularly since the centre of power in the BBC remained in central London in Broadcasting House, which was also the headquarters of radio: many people in radio were suspicious and jealous of the new medium.

Thus television news was gravely hampered by being controlled by the editorial decisions of radio. Television news had, for instance, to follow the same running order of stories as radio bulletins. There were fears about newsreaders appearing in vision because of the dangers of personalising the news; there were doubts about the use of pictures, which it was felt would in some way trivialise the content of the newscast. Puritan patriarchy resurrected these objections when the first female newsreader was proposed, whose sexual attributes would, it was argued, distract the male viewers and rob the newscast of its authority.

Although audiences continued to grow as sets became cheaper, the tone of BBC television was middle class and London-based. By ignoring the regions and showing reluctance to shed its middle-class Southern image the BBC left its centralised broadcasting monopoly wide open for challenge.

The Arrival of Commercial Television

The BBC continued to enjoy its television monopoly until 1955 when, as a result of the 1954 Television Act, commercial television came into existence in Britain. The Act was the result of an unparalleled campaign by advertisers and other commercial interests and of a fierce political battle in which opinion within the Labour and Conservative parties was curiously divided. Labour was inclined on the one hand to defend the BBC as a non-profit-making public service and on the other to criticise it for its Establishment image and lack of appeal to the traditional Labour supporters in the working class. The Conservatives were divided between those who defended the BBC in line with the gentlemanly tradition of public service and others who championed commercial television in the name of free enterprise.

In the end Independent Television (ITV), as the first commercial channel was called, was required by an Act of Parliament to operate under public service rules. The Act spelt out that it had to 'inform, instruct and entertain'. It was also expressly required not to 'offend against good taste and decency'. It had to present news with 'due accuracy and impartiality'. It was to observe impartiality in matters of political or industrial controversy or in comments on current public policy, a stipulation which did not exclude properly balanced discussions or debates where persons taking part express opinions and put forward arguments of a political character.

In those days the charter under which the BBC operated did not give such explicit instructions, it being taken for granted that the BBC would not offend. But there appeared to be a certain mistrust of commercial television in the minds of the legislators who feared that programme and policymakers in commercial television, who on the whole came from very different backgrounds from the predominantly Oxbridge-educated BBC staff, might not instinctively know the limits of 'taste and decency'.

As the Act went through Parliament much of the debate concerned the kind of advertising to be allowed. (Reith, by now a lord, proclaimed that the coming of commercial television was comparable to the Black Death.) MPs who had been to the United States were alarmed at the number of commercials on US television and the frequency with which programmes were interrupted. They also saw dangers in sponsorship as practised in the US. Sponsors could use their financial support as leverage to influence programme decisions if, for instance, a programme was critical of the 'product' being advertised. Sponsorship of programmes was therefore prohibited and the Postmaster-General (the minister then responsible for broadcasting) limited the frequency of commercials to 'natural breaks' of approximately every twenty minutes.

The Structure of ITV

The regulatory body set up to oversee ITV was then known as the Independent Television Authority (ITA). It decided to divide the country into a series of franchise areas; in each area there would be a single franchise holder who would contract to supply a television service. This was seen as a way of avoiding the dominance of London, of fostering regional programming and encouraging competition. Applicants who had satisfied the ITA that they were financially sound and had acceptable programme policies were awarded a franchise for which they had to pay a rental to the ITA which in turn gave them the right to draw advertising revenue from their area. They entered into a contract to this effect and were known as 'the contractors'. That contract was renewable after a fixed term of years, the number of which has varied depending on the political and financial circumstances at the time of each franchise bid.

The Early days of ITV

After a shaky start, when commercial television lurched from week to week barely breaking even, ITV quickly became profitable and enormous sums of money were made. STV, the main Scottish franchise-holder, made £52 million in twelve years from a starting capital of £500,000. The chairman of the company was unwise enough to say that a franchise was 'a licence to print money'. Part of the revenue earned by the franchise-holders was being used for other commercial ends than television. The pickings became so great that a Conservative government imposed a levy on the ITV companies: a special tax, over and above income tax, on advertising revenue. Commercial television was too shameless in showing the unacceptable face of capitalism.

This levy was changed in 1974 to become a 66 per cent charge on profits calculated after a fixed fee had already been paid. The levy is still charged to all terrestrial commercial television companies.

Over time, a hierarchy of contractors was formed with big players like Granada, Central, London Weekend, Thames and Yorkshire (not all of whom are still franchise-holders today) at the top. They were the companies who had sufficient advertising revenue and capital to set up production facilities for programme-making. They could produce ratings winners like *Coronation Street* (Granada), *The Bill* or *Blind Date*. As with any uneven distribution of finance and power the smaller companies like Anglia, Border and Tyne Tees, had limited production resources and had to struggle to compete for national airtime. The largest contractors not only had the money to produce programmes but they also charged the other regional companies on the national commercial network a fee for broadcasting them.

The Challenge to the BBC

The arrival of ITV presented an immediate challenge to the BBC. An important example was in the field of news reporting. A separate company, Independent Television News (ITN), wholly owned by the commercial television companies, came on air in September 1955 to provide commercial television with regular news programming. ITN quickly built up a large audience by its use of presenters like Robin Day and Christopher Chataway, the Olympic runner, and by its less formal language and more populist news values. This was symptomatic of a swing in the mass audience away from the BBC whose share of the ratings fell to around 30 per cent – a dangerous state of affairs.

Large profits continued to be made by the programme companies. Despite earlier misgivings over commercial television, however, ITV and BBC seemed compatible, both channels operating well within the boundaries set by the principles of public service broadcasting. The BBC, faced by the professional challenge of ITV, picked up its ratings and a more or less equal share of the available audience. Until the 1960s there was a fairly comfortable duopoly with ITV functioning under a Television Act and the BBC under the terms of its Royal Charter.

BBC2

A major change in the picture came about when the BBC was allowed in 1964 to open up a second channel, BBC2. Its inauguration coincided with the adoption of a new lines standard – 625 lines instead of 405

– which gave a better picture and facilitated the adoption of colour. The proclaimed aim of the new channel was to accommodate programmes that could not find a place in the BBC1 schedules and thus to provide an alternative service. Today the relationship is symbiotic. A system of cross-trailing from one channel to the other is designed to retain the audience and prevent it from switching elsewhere. Innovation would have to wait until a new commercial channel came on the air in 1982: Channel 4.

The Coming of Channel 4

From 1955 to 1982 commercial television was broadcast on only one channel – Channel 3 – which carried ITV programmes. In the 1970s, however, the government announced that there was to be a new channel, Channel 4. The nature of the future channel was debated by a committee on broadcasting set up by the Labour government and chaired by Lord Annan, vice-chancellor of London University.

The committee's report showed that they were aware of the contemporary debate in Britain and elsewhere in western Europe concerning the ownership of the media and access to them. It was a debate that had its roots in the questioning of social structures which lay behind the radical movements of 1968. An important part was played in the UK by the Free Communications Group (FCG) which attacked the bureaucracy of the BBC and the financial empires of the big ITV companies. It called for the administrative and editorial control of the media by those who worked in them and for free access to the air. One legacy of this debate was the widely canvassed proposal that when a fourth channel was set up it should be as a publisher – that is to say, subject, like a book, newspaper or magazine publisher, only to the laws of the land on such matters as libel, obscenity, contempt of court and infringements of the Official Secrets Act.

The Annan Report

The terms of this report, which appeared in 1977, reflected the committee's consciousness of important changes in society which found expression in hostility to the traditional organs of the State and to those in any institution charged with its governance. In terms of broadcasting this had increased the tension between the new generation of programme makers and the broadcasting authorities and 'even more dramatically between the authorities and the government'.

The recommendations produced by the committee were rather less radical than its social analysis might have led one to expect. However, one important proposal was that the new fourth channel should be run by an 'Open Broadcasting Authority', that it should encourage productions which said something new in new ways and that the Open Broadcasting Authority should operate more as a publisher of programmes and should in no way be responsible for their content. In this, and in the proposal that there should be more access programmes which allowed individuals or groups to put forward their views in their own way, it is possible to see some input from the thinking of the FCG. The findings of the committee affirmed the public service ethos; but they also marked the end of an era when the concepts of public service were synonymous with the political consensus.

Before any action could be taken on the committee's recommendations the Labour Government fell in the 1979 election ushering in a Conservative government that remained in office for more than a generation. Some of the committee's recommendations nevertheless had an important influence on the future shape of broadcasting when the new Conservative administration turned to the problem. The government's decisions were set out in the Broadcasting Act 1980 which reflected differences of opinion within the Conservative party on the role of television. On the one hand the traditionalists represented by Whitelaw, Margaret Thatcher's Home Secretary, the man who at that time was responsible for broadcasting, favoured public service. On the other hand, there were Tories who supported a free market economy who wanted broadcasting to be considered as an industry.

Clearly the Conservative government did not take on board the Annan Committee's view that 'an increase in the number of channels does not necessarily lead to an increase in the range of programme services.' Nor did it accept the recommendation that the Fourth Channel should be run by an Open Broadcasting Authority operating as a publisher. What was accepted was that the new channel should encourage productions which said something new in new ways and that the BBC and the ITV should be more willing to buy programmes from independent producers. This idea had been lobbied for by the Independent Programme Producers' Association (IPPA).

The Funding and Structure of Channel 4

In 1980 the new channel was at last set up under the regulatory authority at that time, the Independent Broadcasting Authority (previously the

ITA), as a subsidiary company of the Authority to run a national channel – not a regional one like ITV – which would be financed by subscriptions from the ITV programme companies. They in return had the right to sell advertising time on Channel 4 in their own franchise areas. This arrangement did not please the advertisers who had hoped that competition for advertising revenue between the ITV companies of Channel 3 and Channel 4 would benefit them by reducing advertising rates. However Whitelaw took the view that 'broadcasting was not determined primarily' by the needs of the advertisers.

These advertisers were initially nervous about the success of the new channel; they were unsettled by the talk about new programmes, for they prefer long-established formulas with no risk attached to them. The government reflected the advertising lobby's anxiety that the channel would not survive commercially and as a cautionary measure built into the Act a 'safety net ' for Channel 4. Were the channel's revenue to fall below 14 per cent of the combined advertising and sponsorship revenue of ITV (what is called total qualifying revenue or TQR), the ITV companies might be required to support Channel 4. But if the new channel earned over 14 per cent of TQR, 50 per cent of that excess would be paid to ITV. This provision became a bone of contention between Channel 4 and the ITV companies: the channel, far from collapsing, was successful, but the more successful it is the more it must pay to ITV. In 1995 Channel 4 had to pay over £57 million to Channel 3 which, if converted into money for programmes, could have funded a lot of productions.

The new channel had no production facilities of its own apart from a minimum studio capacity. Its first head, Jeremy Isaacs, was determined to avoid the large bureaucracies of the BBC and the big ITV companies which are in part necessary for in-house productions. It was to operate with a small number of commissioning editors, each being responsible for an area of programming.

Channel 4 is a paradoxical phenomenon. On the one hand it has pursued a liberal and innovative policy, filling the gaps left by other channels, to test the frontiers of taste and of political controversy. On the other hand, it is a Thatcherite model par excellence, dependent on a free-for-all among fiercely competing independent production companies, which have been known to allow conditions of work such as deferred payment (until the production has made some money) to no payment, offering the experience of programme making as incentive enough for the thousands of people desperately eager to work in television. The commissioning editors for their part have become, in the course of time, the dispensers of vast patronage.

Channel 4 and its Audience

When Channel 4 started up, the advertisers argued that programmes with only 250,000 viewers were not acceptable. (It is a comment on their criteria that a quarter of a million people is considered a small audience.) But Channel 4's policy was not like that of the other channels of attracting and keeping an audience throughout the evening. What it hoped to achieve was a more selective audience which might be very large for some programmes and relatively small for others. In the course of time the advertisers came to recognise that the audience might be small but was socially and economically up-market; the audience was less bothered about breakfast cereals and washing powders but more interested in large cars, holiday villas, wine and expensive perfumes. Viewers could therefore be targeted by advertisers in what has come to be known as 'niche audiences', small compared to the millions who watched ITV but with money to spend on the specific products advertised on the screen. In advertising language the demographics were good: the audiences were in the ABC1 economic groups and in the lower age range.

The Future of Channel 4

Channel 4 has become so successful that, in a bitter irony, they have become open to the threat of privatisation as a commercially viable concern. In the summer of 1996 a figure representing (or rather substantially overestimating) the value of Channel 4 was published in the press along with rumours that the government were planning to privatise it.

Channel 5

Channel 5 (C5) originally aimed to reach only 70 per cent of the population. The region that loses out is the South-East where the C5 signal could cause interference with French television. It is envisaged that at some point this coverage will be supplemented by a satellite signal.

Channel 5 is in fact going to be the last analogue terrestrial television service in Britain. It is also described as being the last 'free' service of this kind; presumably this means that we can expect future services to be financed by subscription or pay-per-view.

When Channel 5 was first proposed it was clear that it would be a commercial station. The debate was whether it should be a national network or made up of a number of independent and local stations. There was, for instance, a campaign with strong support in Leeds for a local station reflecting the social, economic, cultural and political interests of the community. There were two problems. The first was that this could have meant that in Leeds there was a television station with a close connection to a Labour local administration. This would not be acceptable to the Conservatives who had lost control of most councils. The second problem was connected with finance. The advertising agencies did not believe that there was sufficient local advertising revenue to make the channel viable. There must still be doubts whether there is sufficient advertising revenue available to fund ITV, Channel 4, satellite services and Channel 5. But competition for revenue will be welcomed by the advertisers who can expect lower rates for their commercial spots. It will also mean that the new channel will be run (at least in the beginning) on a much smaller budget than the other terrestrial channels.

Another financial disadvantage that emerged was that the signal set aside for C5 would use the same frequencies as are employed by video-cassette recorders (VCRs). Viewers in the new channel's reception area would no longer be able to record programmes or watch pre-recorded videos. Retuning all these VCRs (nearly ten million of them) would cost C5 up to £60 million.

The new channel's programme director is quoted as saying that she aims at getting long runs of shows at low prices with a total budget of £150 million, which is a quarter of ITV's budget for the year. Like Channel 4, the new channel has no production capacity of its own. Commissioning editors will procure programmes from what has been ominously described as 'a small group of established independent producers'.

Given the restricted coverage of the new channel and its low budget, there was some surprise when David Elstein, who had been the director of programmes for BSkyB and, as he admitted, the most vocal exponent of the merits of the satellite revolution, announced in the autumn of 1996 that he was going to run the new channel. As a new convert to terrestrial television he defends the new channel as a 'national general entertainment service offered to 70 per cent of the nation 'at no cost to the consumer – no hardware, no smartcard, no additional fees, no fiddling with a separate remote control'. The channel's programme and scheduling policies were foreshadowed by his statement that the audience was 'well aware of the advantages of stripped schedules' – that is, with programmes running across the week at the same time of day, 'and [was] responsive to targeted programming' – by which he presumably meant niche television.

5 The Regulatory Bodies

Broadcasting in the United Kingdom is licensed by the government and is controlled by regulatory bodies whose members are government appointees. There is no such regulatory system for the press or publishing – the licensing of newspapers was abolished in the seventeenth century. Why should it be thought necessary to control broadcasting in this way?

Since broadcasting began in the 1920s, the argument has been that access to a scarce public utility had to be controlled, an argument which is becoming harder to sustain with the increasing number of channels; but it is possible to find another motive. From the beginning of broadcasting (in the form of radio), it was felt by politicians that what came over the air was too readily accessible to too many people. Radio and television are media which directly address anyone who can hear or see; it is not necessary to be literate to use them.

An all-pervasive medium like television which is accessible to almost the entire population is on these grounds thought to be one that requires to be controlled. There is a fear which emerges from time to time that the less well-educated or less well-informed could be exposed to and misinterpret material which a better-educated audience would be able to cope with. The argument takes strange forms – such as Churchill's doubt that a programme on the H-bomb could safely be shown to a mass audience.

There is, however, an argument for another kind of regulation, one that would insist that access to the screen should be used both to encourage and foster the diversity of opinions in a democratic and pluralistic society and to resist any attempt by purely economic market forces for determining broadcasting policy.

The Great and the Good

In Britain the men and women who are, in law, responsible for what is seen on television are the governors of the BBC and of the Independent Television Commission, which is responsible for commercial television.

In the case of the BBC the governers must see that it discharges its duties under the Royal Charter and in the case of the ITC that the terms of the Television Act of 1990 (see Chapter 6) are observed by the commercial television companies. They are also charged in the last analysis with the task of making judgements on taste and decency, on political balance and impartiality. The governers have been drawn from the list of 'the great and the good' – or what might more accurately be defined as 'the safe'. This list is kept in Whitehall by the director of the Public Appointments Unit of the Civil Service Department. It contains the names of those citizens who have been recommended to successive governments as dependable enough to be called upon to officiate on government committees of enquiry, on quangos (quasi-autonomous non-governmental organisations), the BBC being the biggest of them all. Over a period of years the choice has frequently but not surprisingly fallen on ex-ambassadors, retired high-ranking civil servants, businesspeople, pillars of the Establishment, the occasional right-wing trade unionist – in short, almost without exception middle-class people who are unlikely to advocate radical policies or to run counter to the consensus to which all the parliamentary parties subscribe.

It was long a convention that the governors of the BBC or of the ITC were not appointed on a party basis; that is to say, a Conservative prime minister would not necessarily appoint a Conservative to a place on either of the boards of governors or to be chairperson of the bodies governing the BBC or ITV. This has sometimes been pointed to as one of the virtues of the British broadcasting system. That system, we are encouraged to believe, has the concept of neutrality and balance enshrined in it. In the Thatcher years, however, when strong Thatcher supporters like the novelist P. D. James or Marmaduke Hussey were made respectively a governor and the chairman of the BBC, it was impossible not to see them as political appointees.

An analysis of the kind of people who have been appointed to the two boards reveals a homogeneity of ideology, codes and conventions which are far from neutral, their fundamental purpose being the continuation of the existing social structures. Some of the most informed and critical views on broadcasting and its role in society have been advanced by academics who are radical and on the Left in politics; but they are unlikely to be appointed to the boards of governors of either the BBC or the ITC. They are too critical of the system.

The way the BBC and the ITC are run – their governance of the broadcasting insitutions – requires examination and reform. The way in which their members are appointed should be open to public scrutiny

– one suggestion is that their appointment would be a task for a parliamentary committee and that membership be extended outside the ranks of the 'great and good'. To implement a reasonable level of accountability the committee would require an annual report from the governors of both the ITC and the BBC.

The Consensus and the Controls

As far as governments and managements are concerned the present control system has operated fairly smoothly for many years. The regulators have worked within the concept of the 'politics of consensus' – the mainstream of political thinking within our bourgeois democracy. The consensus covers what the television authorities and most politicians would define as the centre of the political spectrum – a band of opinion which may, from time to time, shift slightly to left or right, and which may expand or contract according to the political climate at any time. Political ideas that lie outside the mainstream may be discussed but will at the same time be distanced. (Thus a BBC series examining Marxism included no Marxist speaker.)

The consensus also extends to that body of opinion to which it is believed all reasonable citizens subscribe and which covers not only politics but morals and religion, in short, questions of taste and decency which have excluded certain religious faiths, certain attitudes to sexuality, and even certain types of clothes and pop music.

The ideas that make up the consensus are propagated by schools and educational institutions, by the parliamentary parties, by the Church, by official bodies, by the press, by radio and by television – the latter being one of the most widely used sources of information, ideas and social and moral values in our society. Thus the media play an important part in establishing and maintaining the hegemony – the social and political dominance – of a ruling class. The concept of the hegemony was first articulated in the *Prison Notebooks* of Antonio Gramsci, an Italian communist intellectual, whose ideas earned him long years of imprisonment during Italy's fascist regime. Parliamentary democracies are held together, he argued, by a combination of state power, that is, the police and the armed forces, and the ideas that make up the consensus. These dominant beliefs and attitudes act as a glue holding that society together. The consensus encourages us to accept those beliefs and attitudes – and therefore the way our society is organised – as 'natural' and unassailable.

This does not mean that there have not been occasional differences and spats but the instinct of the broadcasters, the boards of governors and the politicians, has been to settle these matters by using the long-established codes for dealing with 'difficult' programmes (see Chapter 7).

The BBC as Prototype

The first broadcasting institution in Britain was the BBC. It started in the early 1920s as a commercial company and became a corporation under a Royal Charter only in 1927. As such it established patterns of behaviour which have persisted ever since.

To understand the kind of relationship developed by the BBC to the government of the day it is instructive to look at its behaviour during the crucial year of 1926 -- the year of the General Strike. Churchill, who was Home Secretary at the time, wished to commandeer the British Broadcasting Company (as it then was); this was resisted by the Conservative prime minister, Stanley Baldwin. His view was that the BBC was in safe hands and that Mr Reith, its general manager, would know what to do. He must also have been aware that the chairman of the Conservative party lived next door to Reith and that he had installed a couple of telephone lines from his office to the BBC's London station. Reith needed no persuasion to support the government for, as he put it in a memorandum to his senior staff after the strike, he saw the BBC as being 'for the government in this crisis' because ' the government . . . was acting for the people'. Apparently 'the people' did not include the strikers who, by withdrawing their labour, had ceased to be part of 'the people' and had been rejected by society. (A more vicious formulation led Margaret Thatcher in the miners' strike of 1984 to talk about 'the enemy within'.)

When the Archbishop of Canterbury offered to broadcast an ecumenical message to both sides in the strike Reith consulted the prime minister who was content for Reith to decide who and what was broadcast. The archbishop did not get on air. Nor was Ramsay MacDonald, the Labour leader, given a broadcast voice. Reith in his private diary was very frank: 'They [Baldwin and his government] want to be able to say that they did not commandeer us [the BBC], but they know that they can trust us not to be really impartial.' It is no coincidence that in July of that year Parliament agreed to change the BBC's status with a Royal Charter or that Reith was knighted in the January Honours list for 1927.

The Role of the Establishment

The importance of this episode, from a period when there was only radio and no television, is that it illustrates the deference of the BBC when making delicate political judgements to the perceived wishes of the government. This process has been facilitated by close links which have traditionally existed between the BBC and the Establishment – that group predominantly composed of men whose professional careers have frequently been connected and who share the same educational backgrounds, the same career structures, the same social attitudes. Thus in the post-war years the chairman of the board of governors was Sir Alexander Cadogan, who had been the head of the Foreign Office while the director general was General Sir Ian Jacob, who had been a secretary to Churchill's war cabinet. In more recent times the chairman was Sir Marmaduke Hussey whose wife, the former Lady Susan Waldegrave, is a lady-in-waiting to the Queen, and the sister of William Waldegrave, the chief secretary to the Treasury.

The Independent Television Commission (ITC)

When commercial television was introduced in 1955 it was provided with a Board of Governors (also drawn from among the 'great and good') the title of which has changed from time to time in response to changes in its powers and functions. It began as the Independent Television Authority (ITA), a title which annoyed the BBC because it seemed to suggest that the BBC was not independent. It was responsible for awarding licenses to the companies who formed the commercial Independent Television Network (ITV). It was also (as the BBC always has been) legally 'the broadcaster' and as such responsible for the output of the network. When commercial radio arrived it became the Independent Broadcasting Authority (IBA).

The IBA was felt in the early years to have been too careful of the interests of the programme contractors, too reluctant to intervene on programme policy and scheduling. Its powers were therefore strengthened in the 1964 Television Act. It then assumed responsibility for the overall planning of the ITV schedule, for the programme policies of the companies, and for enforcing the principles of public service. It also exercised censorship in that it could at any stage of a production from the first proposal to the final edit ask for and impose changes. It also banned programmes. A celebrated case was the banning – before it was made – of a Granada programme *South of the Border* which proposed to examine the question of Ulster as seen from the Irish Republic.

Following the Television Act 1990 the IBA changed its title to the Independent Television Commission (ITC) and underwent further changes in its powers and role. Although still responsible in the last analysis for regulating the network it is no longer 'the legally accountable broadcaster'. The commercial companies, who have come together to form the ITV Association, are now 'the broadcasters' and as such responsible in law for what they broadcast.

Broadcasting Standards

Over and above the BBC and ITC boards there is now a statutory organisation set up to monitor broadcasting and deal with complaints concerning all broadcasting bodies, including satellite and cable services, operating in the United Kingdom. It is the Broadcasting Standards Commission (BSC) which, although it has no regulatory powers, can advise the broadcasters, its main task being to deal with complaints. Until its creation the BBC and the ITC were judge and jury in their own cases when dealing with complainants and there was no neutral body to which viewers or programme makers who, for instance, had been subject to censorship, could appeal. The members of the commission are once again drawn from that same list of stalwart citizens who can be relied upon to uphold the status quo. The chairman (*sic*) of the BSC is the wife of a former Conservative Foreign Secretary and her deputy is a peer.

Although the BSC has no regulatory powers it has nevertheless drawn up a code of practice to which broadcasters are 'required to give general effect in their own codes and guidelines'. The code, which covers such topics as the portrayal of violence, sex and decency, stereotyping and 'swearing', is a remarkably liberal document which says, for instance, when discussing violence that 'any shrinking from the retelling of savage and bitter truths about the world does the audience a substantial disservice'. On the question of taste and decency it notes that there is 'a long-standing tradition . . . .challenging or deliberately flouting good taste and decency for the purpose of entertainment. This tradition has its legitimate place in broadcasting.' In wider terms it believes that respect for the audience must be balanced by the right to experiment and a challenge to conventions.

In a not untypical month in 1995 the commission received 69 complaints: 21 dealt with 'taste and decency', only five dealt with violence and nine with sex and sexuality. Of these only four were upheld and another two upheld in part. Research carried out by the BSC points to more concern on the part of the audience concerning violence and bad language and less about sex. Broadcasters who have been criticised by the BSC can be required to publish the findings of the commission in the press or on air.

Advertising Controls

The Broadcasting Act requires the ITC to draw up a code of standards and practice for commercials on terrestrial television and any satellite television signal sent up from the UK.

The code is interpreted by the Broadcast Advertising Clearance Centre (BACC) which takes on this task not only on behalf of the ITV companies but also Channel 4, BSkyB and other commercial broadcasters. It sees advertisements in script form and views the tapes before they are passed for transmission. It is a process the centre describes as 'a form of self-regulatory consumer protection', a case of 'clearance rather than control'. The commercial television companies, the centre's *Notes of Guidance to Advertisers* explains, on the one hand 'have no desire to see revenue lost as a result of unnecessarily restrictive attitudes' and on the other are worried about 'misleading, harmful or tasteless' advertising that might devalue the media.

What is foremost in the minds of those responsible for administering the ITC code is the familiar fact that television penetrates into family homes, that the viewers watching the commercials may have differing attitudes determined by their age, their social status, their cultural and religious frontiers. The *Notes* are therefore an attempt to lay down the parameters of public taste. It is a difficult task demanding by definition an awareness of oppression and exploitation and the subtleties of cultural representations that perpetrate social and economic injustice. The BACC spells out its guidelines in painstaking detail, including the kind of music that can be used and the kind of visual effects that are permitted, for example, subliminal messages are banned.

Despite warnings against the portrayal of women as sex objects 'or mere adjuncts to the sale of goods' a surprising number of advertisements reach our screens which objectify women in just this way. The *Notes* do not challenge the traditional division of labour between the sexes, rather it counsels against representing women in traditional roles as doing work of little or no value or as 'simple-minded'. This has moved advertising on only to the point where women who still wash whiter, cook more tastily, shop more judiciously for anything from breakfast cereal to cars are bright, witty and often just leaving for work outside the home. Regulations applying to children range from not showing dangerous behaviour such as tunnelling in the sand to not encouraging bad behaviour as in 'bad manners'. Commercials must avoid offending any ethnic group, must not be guilty of ageism, and must respect religious sensibilities.

It is a sign of how society has changed that condoms and tampons may now be advertised and smoking may not. One positive ruling is that commercials may not suggest 'that menstruation is in any way unclean or shameful'. However television commercials for sanitary protection may only go out when children are presumed to be out of the way – between 9.00 a.m. and 4.00 p.m. and 9.00 p.m. and 6.00 a.m. during school terms and only after 9.00 p.m. during holidays and weekends. Where contraceptives are concerned, Channel 4 viewers are considered to be less shockable (more sophisticated?) than ITV viewers. Contraceptives may be advertised after 7.00 p.m. on Channel 4 but on ITV only after 9.00 p.m.

6　The Charter and the Act

The Royal Charter

The Royal Charter under which BBC Television, like BBC radio before it, operates has been seen by some as being a guarantee of quality, rather like the cachet bestowed on firms which 'by appointment' supply groceries and wine to the Queen, whereas commercial television, set up by an Act of Parliament, did not have the same royal stamp of approval. But such thinking was a snobbish relic from the days when the BBC enjoyed a monopoly and liked to think of itself as 'the national instrument of broadcasting'. Vestiges of this attitude have lingered, to the corporation's cost. Indeed it is only since 1996 that the Queen's Speech has no longer been produced solely by the BBC.

The importance of the Charter is that it lays down the conditions under which the BBC functions and the rules by which it has to abide. It is renewed from time to time -usually at an interval of ten years. Although the fundamental definition of the BBC's role as a public service institution has remained the same across the years the details of the Charter have varied.

The latest Charter, which runs from 1996 to 2006, begins with a royal rigmarole:

ELIZABETH THE SECOND by the Grace of God of the United Kingdom of Great Britain and Northern Ireland and of Our other Realms and Territories Queen, Head of the Commonwealth, Defender of the Faith:

TO ALL TO WHOM THESE PRESENTS SHALL COME, GREETING!

WHEREAS on the twentieth day of December in the year of our Lord One thousand nine hundred and twenty-six by Letters made Patent under the Great Seal, Our Royal Predecessor His Majesty King George the Fifth granted unto the British Broadcasting Corporation a Charter of Incorporation:

. . . AND WHEREAS it has been represented to Us by Our right trusty and well beloved Counsellor Virginia Bottomley Our Secretary of State for the National Heritage, that it is expedient that the Corporation should be continued for the period ending on the thirty-first day of December Two thousand and six.

. . . AND WHEREAS in view of the widespread interest which is taken by our Peoples in broadcasting services and of the great value of such services as means of disseminating information, education and entertainment We believe it to be in the interests of Our Peoples of Our United Kingdom . . . that there should be an independent corporation which should provide broadcasting services

and so on.

The short and the long of it is that the BBC as a public service organisation takes on certain duties, the most important being to inform, educate and entertain. The twelve governors are responsible for the overall strategy and policies of the organisation. They traditionally appoint the director general who runs the BBC from day to day and who, as editor-in-chief, is responsible, among other things, for its programme output. This division of powers was fought for by the BBC's founder, John Reith, who felt that there should not be too much meddling by governors in the day-to-day work of the professional broadcasters.

The new Charter registers an extension of the governers' powers, for they will now also appoint their deputies as well as other members of the board of management, which is composed of powerful executives; they will also make other key appointments as they see fit. This autocratic measure is meant to ensure that the programme policies are in suitably safe hands.

The Governors are also responsible for the appointment of advisory bodies and of the National Broadcasting Councils for Scotland, Wales and Northern Ireland, the members of which naturally represent the same consensual point of view as that of the governors themselves.

The Agreement

Just as important as the Charter is the accompanying Agreement between the BBC and the Secretary of State responsible for broadcasting. At various times the minister responsible for broadcasting has been the Postmaster General, the Home Secretary, the Secretary of State for Trade and Industry and is presently the Secretary of State for National Heritage – changes which reflect the view adopted by various governments as to the nature and importance of broadcasting: is it a social institution, a cultural activity or an industry.

The Agreement now in force lays down that the BBC shall have two television programme services but may, if it wishes, increase their number. In line with government proposals, the BBC is allowed to provide facilities for digital television. On the programme side it is required to maintain high general standards and to offer a wide range of subject matter.

The Licence Fee

On the financial side the Agreement lays down what the BBC will receive from the licence revenue, which is fixed at a figure determined by the government. When the BBC was set up as a corporation the licence fee was paid by the owners of radio sets; today, due to the impossibility of keeping track of transistor and car radios, it applies only to the owners of television sets. The present agreement lays down that the BBC will receive the whole of the licence fee. This has not always been the case. The Treasury for a long time withheld a large part of the proceeds of the tax and could still at any time change the arrangement. In the past sometimes up to a third of licence revenues has been kept in the Treasury coffers. The government in other words has the power to retain whatever percentage it sees fit of the total licence fee revenue. It can also increase or decrease the size of the fee. Until recently the government took approximately 12 per cent of the gross revenue for various expenses incurred in connection with the collection of the fee from set-owners.

The funding of the BBC by the licence fee, supplemented by the BBC's earnings from programme sales, merchandising and publishing, has been under threat for two reasons. First, Margaret Thatcher, who deeply disliked and distrusted the BBC, wanted to turn it into a commercial broadcasting organisation; second, while the tax will continue to be levied from all set-holders, the BBC's audience share is bound to fall given the increasing number of competing channels, the expansion of cable and satellite broadcasting and the explosion of digital channels. True, John Major's government has backed away from Thatcher's privatisation plans and has said the licence fee will continue to be levied. However, if the audience share is eroded by new competitors the question of how the BBC is to be financed may become active once more.

The fact that the present situation is not guaranteed for all time is demonstrated by the inclusion of an extremely important clause in the new Charter which allows the BBC to provide television and other services 'funded by advertisement, subscription, sponsorship and pay-by-view systems'. The implications are far-reaching. The BBC has already embarked on a very limited night-time subscription service (BBC Select) for certain professions (nurses, doctors, lawyers, etc.) when the screens would otherwise be blank. In future, the BBC will be free to develop other subscription services as a source of revenue. This runs contrary to the concept at the basis of public service broadcasting that programmes should be universally available to all licence-holders. It would encourage the emergence of a two-tier system of broadcasting governed by the ability to pay. Moreover, were the BBC to come to rely on any of the methods of funding listed -- advertising, sponsorship,subscription, pay-per-view -- the argument against the continuance of the licence fee would be greatly strengthened. Politicians would argue against the continuance of the licence as a regressive tax. This clause could open the door to the privatisation of the BBC as another commercial broadcasting organisation and is apparently a possibility from which neither the government nor the BBC shrinks.

The figure at which the licence fee is set -- in 1996 it went up to £89.50 per annum -- must be negotiated with the government from time to time (especially in a period of inflation and rising costs). This means that the minister responsible for broadcasting effectively holds the BBC's purse-strings. In the past there have been occasions when the BBC has transgressed in the eyes of the government, for example, by airing too many critical programmes or otherwise annoying the government politically. It therefore found it more difficult to persuade the minister to increase the size of the licence fee. In other words, the setting of the licence fee is an important control mechanism.

There is one curious consequence of the fact that the BBC is financed by the revenue from the sale of television licences and not from direct government funding. Technically, this means that it is not spending public money and the minister therefore takes no public responsibility for the BBC's policies and does not answer questions in Parliament about them.

The Rules of the Game

Whereas the Charter deals with broad principles, the Agreement is prescriptive. Apart from providing a public service of information, education and entertainment, BBC programmes must stimulate, support and reflect the diversity of cultural activity in the United Kingdom, provide 'comprehensive, authoritative and impartial coverage of news and current affairs,' and provide 'wide-ranging coverage of sporting and other leisure interests'. It must show programmes of an educational nature and encourage a 'high standard of original programmes' for children and young people. Other programmes should reflect the lives and concerns of both local and national audiences and include a range of programmes made outside London and the South-East.

Its duties include 'the provision of a balanced service' covering 'a wide range of subject matter'. It must serve the tastes of different audiences and 'show concern for the young' by placing programmes at appropriate times, a reference to the 9.00 p.m. watershed after which 'grown-up' programmes may be shown. It must treat controversial subjects 'with due accuracy and impartiality'.

The terms of the current agreement point to a tightening of controls. Thus controversial subjects must be presented with 'due accuracy and impartiality, both in the corporation's news services and in the more general field of programmes dealing with matters of public policy or of political or industrial controversy'. When conditions are spelt out in this way it points to two things: sensitivity on the part of a government increasingly under attack from all sides, and willingness on the part of the BBC to acquiesce in terms which are likely to inhibit journalistic endeavour.

Good Taste and Decency

The Agreement also stipulates that the BBC must not include in its programmes 'anything which offends against good taste or decency'. This is a new requirement. A similar injunction appears in the Television Act which applies to ITV, the commercial television channel; but it had apparently been assumed until recently that the BBC would instinctively exercise proper judgement in this field. But what is 'decency' and what is 'good taste'? Both of these concepts are difficult to define because they are not the same for different sections of the audience: the ideas of many viewers on the subject are not likely to coincide with those of the Board of Governors. 'Taste' is something that is constantly changing along with changes in our society and what the viewing public will accept. Images now appear on our screens without protest from the public which thirty years ago would have caused a scandal. Audience research shows that the viewing public is more upset by bad language than by sex and violence, which is odd in a society where four-letter words are in everyday use.

Who is to say where the line is to be drawn in matters of taste? Are the BBC's governors qualified by their social origins, their age and education to make these judgements on our behalf? What exactly is meant by 'impartiality'? The answer depends on where one stands politically.

The Gagging Clause

An extremely important part of the Agreement comes under the heading of defence and emergency arrangements. Specifically one clause under this heading states that the Secretary of State may 'from time to time' request the corporation to transmit 'certain material'. This is usually taken to mean that the government would have the right in the event of some national crisis or local emergency to make the BBC broadcast information or advice. The following paragraph states the converse of this. It says that the Secretary of State 'may from time to time . . . require the Corporation to *refrain* . . . from broadcasting any matter or class of matter' specified by the government. The BBC has the right 'to announce or refrain from announcing' that what is in fact a gagging clause has been applied. In other words it might (though it seems unlikely because it would be a politically bold act) simply put a caption on the screen saying: 'The scheduled programme will not be transmitted on the orders of the Minister responsible for broadcasting.'

This clause, the terms of which are replicated in the Television Act, clearly provides a mechanism for censorship and is a powerful deterrent even though it has seldom been used. Governments prefer to obtain their ends by other less public means – by off-the-record talks, meetings where no minutes are taken and by understandings and agreements. It is a mutually maintained fiction, benefiting both the governors of the broadcasting industry and the government alike, that television within the UK cannot be silenced or swayed and that authoritarian censorship does not exist.

7 The Growth of Government Intervention

As we have seen, the tradition of co-operation and collusion between the governors of the BBC and the government of the day worked well in a world when these powerful figures were drawn from the same class, background and education. After the Second World War, and particularly during the 1960s, unquestioning respect for the previous generation had broken down and with it the sanctity of the institutions they controlled. The effects of this within broadcasting meant that programme makers, and on some occasions BBC governors were not in automatic agreement with the government over what constituted 'good taste and decency' and the 'national interest'. The result has been an increasingly overt governmental intervention, most particularly during the years of the Thatcher government.

That Was The Week That Was

That Was The Week That Was (*TW3*) was the first venture into political satire on British television in the 1960s and it was considered a 'difficult' if not to say dangerous programme. In the 1990s we have had the savage wit of *Spitting Image* and *The Rory Bremner Show* but *TW3* was unique in directing its fire at politicians, judges, royalty, the Church and other sacred cows of the Establishment.

Although a Conservative Party official condemned the programme as having 'a general bias that was left wing, socialist and pacifist', *TW3* was 'radical' only in the choice of its targets. Its politics were those of insiders who understood the mechanisms of the Establishment and were prepared to mock them but not to attack the system as a whole. Where the team blundered was in delivering their message in terms of schoolboy humour and thus laying themselves open to attacks from the Board of Governors.

Despite the BBC's strong financial position at the time, the governors were from the start nervous and deprecated what they saw as lapses in taste. They began to report from their contacts in Parliament that some government ministers were becoming increasingly sensitive about the damage such lampooning would do to their position and image. One BBC governor clearly identified with these ministers, rather than with the thousands of viewers who, voting with their feet, left the pubs early to catch the programme; he threatened to resign over the issue. Wearied by continuous criticisms of the programme by members of the board, the director general, who had been a strong supporter of the programme, decided to take it off the air after a run of a year. The lame explanation given was that since there was a general election in the near future it would be wrong to continue with a programme of this kind.

Self-censorship: *The War Game*

The War Game, a BBC drama documentary on the effects of a nuclear attack, produced in 1965, posed a much more serious problem. The effects of nuclear war on the civilian population was obviously a 'sensitive' issue. The control system of political pressure and management compliance quickly got to work.

This was not the first time that a programme on nuclear warfare had caused difficulties for the BBC. In the 1950s work had begun on a radio documentary on the hydrogen bomb. Ministers, alarmed at the prospect of a programme which would speak of civilian casualties, demanded to see scripts. After a certain reluctance on the part of the BBC, meetings were held at the Ministry of Defence with the chairman, who had been head of the Foreign Office, and the director general, who had been military secretary to Churchill's wartime cabinet. It was explained that while the ministry

> did not desire to keep the public in entire ignorance; on the other hand they did not want to stimulate the feeling so easily accepted by the British people because it agreed with their natural laziness in these matters, that because of the terrible nature of the hydrogen bomb there was no need for them to take part in home defence measures . . .

Close liaison on the subject between the BBC and the Ministry of Defence was agreed to be a more satisfactory and practical solution than that the government should try to lay down precise rules in writing. The gentleman's agreement was reaffirmed. The programme was never made.

Once bitten, twice shy: the managers of the BBC reacted with some trepidation to *The War Game*, which was admitted to be an extremely impressive film. The chairman of the board of governors at the time was Lord Normanbrook who had been secretary to the Cabinet and head of the Civil Service; he therefore had contacts at the centre of political power.

Normanbrook took soundings in Whitehall and a private showing was arranged for representatives of the Home Office (which was responsible for civil defence), the chiefs of staff of the Armed Forces and some senior BBC executives. There were a few minor reservations on the part of the officials but they were not prepared to decide that the film should not be shown. One courageous senior BBC executive was of the opinion that 'people who live as we do under the shadow or under the protection – however you care to put it – of the nuclear bomb should have a realistic idea of such a bomb . . . On what basis' he asked, 'could it be said that it is wrong even to attempt to make a film with this aim?' His view did not prevail. The government preferred to leave it to the BBC to be its own censor. The programme was not shown until 1985, close to the anniversary of the bombing of Hiroshima.

The Question of Ulster

Northern Ireland had long presented the broadcasters and in particular the BBC with policy problems. They can be summed up by the question: What is the role of public service broadcasting, which is based on the idea of a consensus, in a society where such a consensus does not exist? The dilemma was formulated in another way by a BBC executive in Northern Ireland who said that the BBC was expected to stand by the government 'in the national interest' but Northern Ireland had at that time two governments – Westminster and the Ulster parliament in Stormont. In his view the broadcasting media should function as a 'fourth estate', distinct from the executive, the legislature and the judiciary, and should be allowed to decide 'within the limits of responsibility' what to publish. In the situation of the time this was a bold statement; this same BBC executive was to become the object of Margaret Thatcher's ire when he suggested at the time of the Falklands War that there was an Argentinian case to be heard as well as a British one.

In fact, the BBC in Northern Ireland had for many years in its programming and reporting avoided anything that might upset the

Unionists who complained bitterly at any reporting of Republican activities. Crews and reporters from London who did not know the local rules were not welcome. When the Troubles started, the BBC's policy became one of censorship. When in August 1969, Catholics were burnt out of their homes in the Falls Road by Protestants, reports by the BBC in Belfast, as one BBC journalist confessed, 'gave no indication of who the refugees were'. The public 'was not to know who was attacking whom'. *The History of Broadcasting in the United Kingdom*, the official history of the BBC, admits that 'independent reporting was made almost impossible because of Northern Irish sensitivities', that is, Unionist sensitivities.

It was clear from early on the role the government expected broadcasters to play in the conflict between the IRA and the British authorities. In November 1971 the Minister for Posts and Telegraphs Christopher Chataway publicly announced that 'impartial' reporting representing the IRA versus either the Unionist government or the British Army was not required. The chairman of the ITA, Lord Aylestone, declared 'Britain is at war with the IRA in Ulster and the IRA will get no more coverage than the Nazis would have done in the last war.' The chairman of the BBC was more restrained but agreed that 'between the British Army and the gunmen the BBC is not and cannot be impartial'.

This agreement between State and broadcasters did not prevent an impasse only a month later when a two-and-a-half-hour current affairs programme, *The Question of Ulster*, was proposed, in which a wide range of Ulster politicians were to take part. It attracted a direct attack from the Home Secretary, despite the fact that no IRA members were to be interviewed. The pressure was immense, the BBC's Board of Governors panicked and there was a campaign against the programme in the Tory press. Yet the programme went ahead and was seen by 7.5 million viewers, most of whom were in favour of the attempt to discuss the situation in Northern Ireland. On this occasion, in the very important continuing tug-of-war between professional judgements and the pressures to conform to government desires, the professionals won.

By 1979 the situation had changed. The Prevention of Terrorism Act had been rushed through Parliament as a response to the Birmingham bombings. Section 11 of the Act contained significant legal constraints for British television. Thus, in 1988, Margaret Thatcher had the power to rule that the voice of any Sinn Fein member, a legally elected political party, must be banned from the airwaves. Her justification for this was that these voices would give offence to the British public. The public was then treated to the farcical spectacle of Sinn Fein representatives having their words spoken by actors, who earned handsomely as a result.

Open Intervention

Margaret Thatcher's rise to power ushered in a decade of ever-increasing pressure on the media. The era of the 'quiet chat', of the attempts at negotiation and of the squeamishness of government to censor publicly British broadcasting was at an end. From 1979 onwards, the Thatcher government not only wielded the existing veto contained in the Agreement and reinforced by the Official Secrets Act, but introduced new legislation and police intimidation to curb the freedom of the broadcasting organisations.

Thatcher's hostility to the broadcasters flared into open antagonism during the Falklands War, over the escalating problems in Ireland, over internal strife. Most particularly during the miner's strike of 1984/5, broadcasters and government were brought into consensus once again. This apparent coalescence did not prevent continued attempts by the Thatcher government to curb the independence of the BBC.

Margaret Thatcher had not been prime minister for more than a few months before she sought to prosecute the BBC under Section 11 of the Prevention of Terrorism Act. The BBC's *Tonight* programme interviewed representatives of the Irish National Liberation Army, an organisation which shortly afterwards was declared illegal. The Attorney-General was asked to investigate the possibility of legal action against the BBC. Footage shot by a team from the BBC's public affairs programme, *Panorama*, of an IRA roadblock (ill-advisedly mounted for the benefit of the cameras) roused Margarert Thatcher to public fury, rebuking the BBC and ordering them to put their 'house in order'. The police entered BBC premises to seize the film, an unprecedented move marking a complete break from the previous collaboration between broadcasters and the State. It also marked a willingness on the part of government to restrict television's freedom to report. The following year, the statement from Attorney-General Sir Michael Havers, that the BBC had contravened Section 11 of the Prevention of Terrorism Act in both cases, and was therefore liable to prosecution was yet another crack of the government's whip.

Death on the Rock

The readiness of the Thatcher government to intervene when it felt a programme might raise questions about government policies was demonstrated when Thames Television (which held the London weekday franchise) made a documentary programme called *Death on the Rock*. This was an investigation into the circumstances in which the SAS shot down three members of the IRA in Gibraltar in March 1988. The official story was that the two men and a woman, when challenged by the security forces, had made movements that led the SAS members to believe that their lives were threatened. In fact the dead were unarmed. There was a possibility, in the words of the right-wing MP Enoch Powell, that the SAS had committed 'deliberate, cold-blooded, pre-meditated murder'.

Nevertheless a team of journalists from Thames put together a programme which the Ministry of Defence was aware of and which cast strong doubts on the official version. Two days before it was due to go on air, the Foreign Secretary wrote to the chairman of the IBA asking him to postpone the showing of the programme until after the inquest on the incident in Gibraltar on the grounds that it might prejudice the proceedings. The IBA sought legal advice and decided there were no grounds for holding up the programme which duly went out and was greeted by headlines in the press like 'Fury over SAS' and 'Trial by TV' (*Daily Mail*), 'Storm at SAS Telly Trial' (*The Sun*), 'TV Slur on SAS' (*Daily Star*) and 'Defiant ITV angers Ministers' (*Daily Telegraph*). There was a prolonged debate inside and outside Parliament.

Some weeks later, when one of the interviewees withdrew his statement, claiming he had been pressurised, the IBA decided that an inquiry into the making of the programme was called for. Lord Windlesham, who conducted the inquiry along with a QC, had in his time been a Conservative whip in the Lords and a Home Office and Northern Ireland minister. He had the important advantage of having worked in television for several years. The inquiry report concluded that the programme had been 'a lighting conductor for the intense feelings the Gibraltar shootings evoked in the minds of the British public'. It was 'a child of its time . . . troublesome and valued simultaneously'. As a programme it was 'trenchant and avoided triviality'. Those who made it acted in good faith. There was no serious criticism of the way it had been made nor of its contents.

An important passage in the report sets out the relationship of broadcasters to government ministers. Some people would argue, it says,

that the mere fact that a minister asks for a programme to be suppressed
on the grounds that it would be 'injurious to the national interest' would
be sufficient reason for compliance. Yet, it goes on, 'the national interest
is no Holy Grail in the exclusive guardianship of the government of
the day . . . A freedom to publish is itself a fundamental and enduring
part of the national interest' just as it is a function of the press and broadcast
media to act as a curb on the abuse of power and administration. All
these things need to be put in the balance when a minister intervenes.
The final responsibility, the report concluded, lies with the broadcasting
authorities, who in this case stood their ground.

8   The Thatcher Years

The Shift to the Right

The 1980s and the premiership of Margaret Thatcher marked a decade
when the political shift to the Right created a climate that encouraged
competitiveness and self-advancement, the survival of the fittest. It had
no room for a social conscience in the form of the *noblesse oblige* of the
old Conservative landowner which stemmed from a belief in the duties
that went with inherited privilege. Thatcher was hostile towards representatives of the old Establishment -- the gentleman's club – not least
because she felt barred from their ranks and, taking umbrage, determined
to create new power networks with herself in command.

The New Right Debate

The change in climate became apparent in the nature of the debates
over broadcasting. In the post-war period these debates had centred on
broadcasting's social effects and cultural importance, in particular, on
the importance of television in forming and changing people's tastes
and in shaping their view of the world through the consensual values
implicit in the programmes. Under Thatcher, the debate shifted to
economics and management. The philosophy of giving free play to market
forces would affect the whole of broadcasting including the BBC.
Concepts like 'downsizing' (getting rid of jobs), and the 'internal
market' would be adopted as they were in other public services. The
era of the accountants had arrived. The way for this era had been
prepared in 1974 when broadcasting had been categorised as a tradeable
service and not as a cultural activity in the European courts; the resultant
legal definition of broadcasting affecting employment, copyright law
and other major concerns became that of an industry.

The Threat to the BBC

In broadcasting the BBC became the target of Thatcher's displeasure
and labelled an effete, elitist organisation with dangerously radical

tendencies. Thatcher had wished to see the BBC commercialised and had accused it at the time of the Falklands War of being insufficiently patriotic. However, there were no complaints from the government about the BBC's coverage of the miners' strike in 1984/85, which was seen as objective and unbiased. In fact the BBC heavily edited scenes of police brutality and on one startling occasion described fleeing miners as having charged the mounted police. The bad old tradition stemming from the 1926 General Strike and Reith's concept of 'objectivty' still held sway.

Thatcher was still unhappy about a public broadcasting service that could behave autonomously and that had, in theory at least, an independent voice. In 1986, when terrorists hijacked a TWA plane, Thatcher accused the BBC of giving the hijackers 'the oxygen of publicity' during a visit to the US. The BBC's reporting on the US bombing of Libya in 1986 was attacked by Norman Tebbit, the Conservative Party chairman, because it gave too much prominence to the deaths of civilians and children. He also objected to the phrase used during *The Nine O' Clock News*: 'We'll be assessing the world reaction to what the Americans have done, and the political repercussions for Mrs Thatcher.' In his opinion the bulletin should have begun with 'We'll be looking at the events that prompted America's retaliation and its chances of success.'

With an overtly hostile prime minister the BBC was under enormous pressure to present a thoroughly reformed profile, both economically and politically. To this end a new breed of managers and governors was appointed whose financial imperatives began to reduce staff levels and cut programme budgets towards the end of the 1980s.

The Role of the Independent Producers

The Annan Report's proposal that the BBC and the commercial companies should be more willing to buy programmes from independent producers and rely less on 'in-house' productions – was something that the Thatcher government had inherited from Labour but that chimed with the prime minister's philosophy. It fitted in well with Thatcher's desire for competition in the market, which would break down the BBC's in-house structure, and her determination to attack the unions, which were strong in both the BBC and ITV. The proposal that the proportion of programmes made by independent producers should be increased was adopted by the Conservative government. In 1986 the Home Secretary (who was then responsible for broadcasting) announced that 25 per cent of new programmes for BBC and ITV should be made by independents.

Initially British Independent production companies were often small and difficult to organise; those who worked in them had no experience of trade unions, were hostile to them and/or unaware of their importance in establishing wages and work practices, in negotiating redundancy pay, and in arguing the case of employees with their employers. From the point of view of the broadcasting organisations, the independents presented the advantage of relieving them of such expenses as national insurance contributions, pensions, paid holidays and union-negotiated wages. The result has been a free-for-all in a ruthless market in which production companies which have been hived off from the BBC and the ITV have an enormous advantage. What is already becoming clear is that the proliferation of small independent producers is giving way, by a process inherent in a capitalist economy, to the formation of fewer and larger units. It has been suggested that this will result in the emergence of four or five main production companies.

Sianel Pedwar Cymru – S4C

A political judgement based on the Conservative party's dwindling foothold in Wales led to one surprising development. William Whitelaw persuaded Thatcher to accept, much against her wishes, the idea of a separate Welsh fourth channel – Sianel Pedwar Cymru (S4C) – to be funded jointly by the BBC and commercial television. This was a political move in the face of strong and persistent pressure from Welsh nationalists, including a threat from one prominent nationalist to fast to the death, and the hold-up of a minister's car in the Welsh mountains. The aim may have been to bolster Conservative fortunes in Wales. It has had, from the Conservative point of view, the less welcome effect of increasing interest in the Welsh language and Welsh identity.

The Role of cable

At the beginning of her administration Margaret Thatcher had made her interest in and support of technological developments clear. She appointed advisers on information technology (IT) and created an Information Technology Unit in the Cabinet Office to deal with advances in this field. Significantly, these advances were seized on primarily as new tools for opening up new markets and increasing potential competition for all terrestrial channels. Cable was identified as one of the areas for expansion.

Though cable companies had been in existence for many years as a means of distributing radio and television signals to 'shadowed' localities, unlike in countries such as the US and Benelux, they did not flourish in the UK because both the BBC and the IBA made sure that the bulk of the population received a good signal. They could not compete with programmes since they had neither the revenue nor the resources to make them and their efforts at local community-based television had petered out. Their technology was old fashioned: bulky copper co-axial cables with limited capacity, much of which was taken up by the BBC and the ITV programmes which they were required to carry.

The Thatcher government believed that, in commercial and industrial terms, cable was an important economic and industrial growth area specifically within the business sector offering opportunities for new forms of entrepreneurial activity. The direct market for equipment alone was estimated at more than £3000 million in 1982. Little consideration was given to the quality of broadcast programming using this medium. Cable was seen as a lucrative market for carrying programmes and films bought from producers both at home and abroad. The cable lobby for its part promised an almost unlimited number of channels, both domestic and foreign, home shopping and interactive viewing. Beyond this there was a vision of a communications system in the future dependent on cable. Initially interest in cable television in Britain was slow. Despite the Conservative hype of the 'unrepeatable opportunity' which developing new cable networks would bring to communications industries and consumer choice alike, British companies were not keen to bear the high cost of actually laying the cables. Between 1983 and 1989, 52 franchises were granted, of which only about a dozen lasted into the 1990s.

The stage is now set for a tussle between cable and satellite television for audiences.

The Radical Rethink

Radical right-wing rethinking about broadcasting was embodied in *The Omega File*, published in 1984. This publication on communications policy, with its suitably sci-fi sounding name, was the work of the Adam Smith Institute. It was remarkable in calling for a free market in broadcasting which would, it was argued, best serve 'consumer choice and the optimisation of opportunities for innovation'. The same market-oriented way of thinking was reflected in the way the electromagnetic spectrum was discussed as a commodity, parts of which could and should be auctioned off to the highest bidder. Gone was the concept of a scarce public resource with the resonances of common ownership.

This mix of radical populism and consumerism was repeated in the criticisms of the licence fee. It was not the social injustice of demanding the same fee from poor and wealthy alike that the report was concerned with, but the complaint that there was no correlation between what the public wished to view/buy and what they were licensed to view/pay for. The result was, the right-wing ideologues argued, that 'the price of viewing is not related to the consumption of the product'.

Within the report's eight proposals were recommendations that BBC1 should be financed by advertising and that, in an effort to decrease regulations, the IBA (the Independent Broadcasting Authority responsible for ITV at the time) be replaced by 'a body more akin to the Federal Communications Commission in the USA' – an organisation that is renowned for the lightness of its regulatory touch and its unwillingness to interfere in programme policies.

Thatcherism produced in broadcasting – as it did in the health service, in education and other public services – important changes in management and organisation: all of them conceived of in terms of markets. Traditionally, the future of broadcasting had been examined by Royal Commissions. In 1985, however, the government set up a committee to look at broadcasting under Professor Peacock who was chosen presumably because he was a liberal (in the sense that he did not favour state intervention or coercion in economic matters) economist. He was also vice-chancellor of Britain's only private enterprise university.

Not surprisingly the Peacock Committee proved to be on the same wavelength as the Adam Smith Institute and it came out for a free market and consumer choice. (It drew back, however, from recommending the privatisation of the BBC.) From this point of view the licence is unsatisfactory not because it is a regressive tax but because one BBC television programme effectively costs the viewer no less or more than another: if the viewer switches off, the BBC does not suffer. The eventual solution would, to this way of thinking, be subscription television which would provide 'a low-cost method for the exchange of information between consumers and suppliers' – that is to say, viewers would express disapproval of programmes by switching off or refusing to pay in the first place. Subscription television means, however, that the less well-off in our society would be unlikely to be able to afford to pay for the service which would certainly, on an annual basis, be more expensive than the cost of the television licence.

Turning its attention to the concept of public service broadcasting the Peacock Committee came up with a definition of it as 'any major modification of purely commercial provision resulting from public policy'. But such intervention interferes with the play of the market forces and produces a system which is second-best to 'a sophisticated market system based on consumer sovereignty'. In this context new technologies like cable and satellite television are welcomed as offering an escape from 'the straitjacket of the duopoly' (i.e. the BBC and ITV) and of giving the consumers control over their own viewing. From this point of view the nature of the programmes provided by the new technologies is not important. Taken to its extreme it would deny the public service concept of the need to inform, educate and entertain.

The New Order of Things

The extent to which the Peacock Committee's report contributed to the government's thinking became apparent in a White Paper released, after some delay, in 1988: *Broadcasting in the '90's: Competition, Choice and Quality*. The title was an epitome of Thatcherite philosophy. Surprisingly, the BBC emerged relatively untouched, and was described officially as 'the cornerstone of British broadcasting'. However, in the report's statement that the government looked forward to the eventual replacement of the licence by subscription, there was a threat to the concept of public service television free at the point of use i.e. without further charge to the viewer.

The IBA was to be replaced by the Independent Television Commission (ITC) which would operate with 'a lighter touch'. Channel 4 was to continue to be innovative but to be self-funding: it would compete for advertising with ITV. A new channel, Channel 5, was to be set up; although defined as 'national in scope', its reach was limited to 70 per cent of the country, as we have seen.

The most significant legacy that Thatcherism left to broadcasting in the 1990s was the plan to auction off the franchises to broadcast on ITV in each area of the United Kingdom and the increasing concept of television as a profit-making industry rather than a programme-making cultural activity.

9   Enter Murdoch – A Cautionary Tale

The Thatcher era drew to a close with a media scramble over direct broadcasting by satellite (DBS) to the British audience. The main player was Rupert Murdoch, an Australian multimillionaire tycoon, who owned television stations and newspapers in three continents. His interventions in television broadcasting in the UK cast light on the strategies and tactics of the large, powerful, and above all, wealthy interests which are competing for control of the television industry and of the communications and media industry of which television is a part.

Global Assets

In the United States, Murdoch owns the Fox TV Network, having adopted American citizenship to be allowed to do so. Fox TV has successfully challenged the long-established NBC, CBS and ABC networks. He also owns the Fox Film Studio (formerly Twentieth Century Fox) which is important as a source of programmes, Fox Interactive TV, Fox Video and a cable channel. But his media holdings do not stop there. He also owns the giant HarperCollins publishing house and a newspaper, the *New York Post*. In Asia, he owns Star TV, which broadcasts by satellite to 54 countries, Star Movies (a satellite pay-channel), the AsiaSat2 satellite system, and is half-owner of an Indian television service carried by Star. In Australia, where he started his career, he owns half the newspapers sold each day. He has stakes in numerous television stations and owns 50 per cent of the leading Australian air carrier.

In the United Kingdom, his News International company owns the *Sun* (circulation 3.9 million), the *News of the World* (circulation 4.7 million), *The Times* and the *Sunday Times*. He was at the forefront of the Thatcherite offensive against organised labour when he moved his papers from Fleet Street to Wapping and successfully challenged the print unions. Most importantly, in terms of television in Britain, he owns 40 per cent of BSkyB.

Early Resistance to Murdoch by the Broadcasting Élite

Murdoch's entry into British broadcasting owed much to the Thatcherite encouragement of expansion in the television industry and to the prime minister's wish to pull the teeth of the *ancien régime* and its broadcasting élite. He was exactly the type of tycoon that Thatcher admired. His newspapers were her solid, strident supporters. United in their desire to undermine the cosy duopoly of the BBC and ITV, Murdoch and Thatcher made a formidable team. She was grateful for his rowdy championship of her in his popular papers and was obviously not troubled by his dominance of the media or by the dangers of cross-media ownership which could concentrate immense power in one man's hands.

Murdoch had not been so encouraged in earlier days. In 1968, after acquiring 7.5 per cent of the voting shares of London Weekend Television, he became a non-executive director. He invested half a million pounds in the company and began to exert his influence, declaring his intention of chairing LWT's executive committee. The Independent Television Authority blocked this move, insisting that a new chief executive, not Murdoch, be appointed. His biographer has written 'Murdoch was angry that the Independent Television Authority had the power to exclude him. He saw it as another example of Establishment hatred of him. He was determined that one day he would break into British television.'

Murdoch Gains a Foothold

Fifteen years later, Murdoch's entry into British television came via a tiny European channel called Satellite Television. Since 1981, the channel had been run on a shoe-string but by 1983 it badly needed an injection of capital. Murdoch provided £10 million and gained a controlling interest in the station, which he renamed Sky.

In the same year negotiations between US business interests and the Luxemburg government culminated in the setting up of Coronet, a medium-powered satellite broadcast system whose signals could be received by smaller dishes. There had been enormous resistance to any US control over European DBS from other European governments, most particularly from France, prompting President Mitterrand's contemptuous dismissal of the Luxemburg project as 'the Coca-Cola satellite'.

The difficulties proved too much for the Americans, who eventually withdrew, but Coronet, renamed Astra, was rescued by a consortium of Luxemburg bankers. In early 1987, Eutelsat, the European organisation responsible for siting satellites, gave Astra a position in space despite complaints from established broadcasters and governments that Astra was an obvious threat to broadcasting standards because of its uncompromising commercial slant. For example, in material to encourage advertisers, children's programmes were commended not on the grounds that television can entertain, inform and educate, but that children today have a considerable amount of disposable income. Despite misgivings Eutelstat did not heed the complaints enough to refuse Sky a position on the Clarke Ring.

Satellite Broadcasting in the UK

Meanwhile, in Britain there had been little development of satellite broadcasting. In 1982 two of the five DBS channels allocated to Britain by WARC 77 (see Chapter 1) were given to the BBC who singularly failed to do anything with them. In April 1986 the IBA invited applications for the 15-year franchise of the remaining three DBS channels. Of the seven received, one was from Murdoch's Sky channel service, already broadcasting to European cable systems. The other groups were united in their aim to keep Murdoch out of British television, fears of a televised *Sun* still strong in the minds of the established television controllers. In the end the franchise was awarded to British Satellite Broadcasting (BSB), a cartel comprising Granada, Anglia Television, Virgin Records and Amstrad. In comparison to Sky, still very much a distribution system rather than a television company, the emphasis of BSB's bid had been on programme-making and quality. The *Sun* unsurprisingly dubbed it 'toffs' telly'.

At first BSB seemed well-placed to develop the satellite channels: Amstrad could manufacture the dishes and receiving equipment, Granada could rent out the equipment, while Anglia and Granada were experienced production companies well-qualified to supply programmes. Despite this structure, BSB was soon running into enormous financial difficulty. By April 1987, the projected costs of launching the service had risen from £500 million to around £650 million making it, together with the Channel Tunnel, one of the biggest risk-capital ventures in the history of the British market. New shareholders came on board – amongst them Reed International, Next and the French company Chargeurs.

There were technical problems as well. BSB was compelled by the terms of the franchise to develop an expensive transmission sytem, D-MAC, thought to produce a better picture than the old PAL system, which is used by terrestrial television in the UK. In May 1987, Amstrad left the project after BSB failed to award Alan Sugar, the creator and controller of Amstrad, exclusive rights to supply the new equipment needed for the innovative system. Sugar not only pulled out of BSB, but went over to manufacture dishes for Sky.

Murdoch was now determined to broadcast to Britain in the teeth of sustained opposition, and during a flamboyant public spectacle in London announced that Sky would soon be available to a British audience. He had leased four transponders on the Astra satellite in November 1988 and was promising to provide 'the dawn of an age of freedom for viewing and freedom for advertising'. Since 1981, government restrictions on newspaper and television cross-ownership had prevented Murdoch from controlling a British broadcasting company. Now he had neatly sidestepped these restrictions by securing a broadcasting position on a satellite outside British jurisdiction.

Murdoch's statement – that 'Broadcasting in this country has for too long been the preserve of the old Establishment that has been elitist in its thinking and in its approach to programming' – echoed much of Margaret Thatcher's old resentments.

Sky v. BSB

The challenge to BSB was blatant. The public would only invest in one system, and the first to deliver would have enormous advantages. Continued technical problems with the D-MAC system was drastically delaying BSB, while Sky, having set up headquarters near Heathrow, was, astonishingly, ready to broadcast by February 1989. In the meantime, buyers from both companies, aware that films and their repeats fill a lot of airtime relatively cheaply (certainly more cheaply than original programmes), were in Hollywood flinging huge sums of money at the major studios for the rights to their film libraries. BSB secured Columbia, MGM/United Artists, Paramount and Universal for a reputed £85 million, while Sky, which already owned Fox, signed up Orion, Touchstone and Warner Brothers for £60 million. Publicity for Sky overflowed in Murdoch's five British newspapers, as did offers for free rental packages.

BSB, objecting to the unfair competition and insisting that Sky be subject to the same legislation as British commercial television which limited newspaper holdings to 20 per cent, put pressure on the Department of Trade and Industry to hold an enquiry. Eighty per cent of MPs polled at the time thought it wrong for one proprietor to have a controlling interest in television, radio and newspapers, but Thatcher's government, massively supported by Murdoch's newpapers at every election since 1979, allowed Sky to continue through lack of specific regulation governing satellite broadcasting.

Murdoch v. the Television Establishment

The international advertising market was initially unenthusiastic about pan-European coverage: only Unilever and Beecham's signed with Sky in the first year despite ridiculously low rates. This pushed Sky, and with it News Corporation, towards insolvency. Murdoch continued to miscalculate the amount of advertising revenue to be had, structuring his finances on a forecast that completely missed the signs that one of the most severe advertising recessions in recent history was imminent.

In the summer of 1989, when Murdoch was invited to deliver the prestigious MacTaggart Lecture at the Edinburgh Television Festival (this itself being an acknowledgement of his importance in British broadcasting), Sky was revealed to be losing his News Corporation £2 million a week. Murdoch's lecture was aggressively confident in spite of these losses; it was a full frontal attack on British public service broadcasting. 'Much of what is claimed to be quality television here is no more than the parading of the prejudices and interests of like-minded people who currently control it', he proclaimed. In what now appears to be the archetypal voice of the 1980s, Murdoch criticised television drama for portraying 'the socially mobile . . . as uncaring; businessmen as crooks; moneymaking . . . to be despised' and declared British television to be 'an integral part of the British disease, hostile to the sort of culture needed to cure that disease'.

Although this was pure doctrine according to Thatcher, it proved a little too strong for William Rees-Mogg, editor of *The Times* and chairman of the Broadcasting Standards Council, who performed some ideological acrobatics by seconding Murdoch's zeal for the open market and at the same time showing a patrician distaste for his populism: 'The market does as Mr Murdoch argues, give people what they want and that is good . . . But I do not want the result to be a McDonald's culture, in which television provides the international fast-food of the mind.' No one pointed out that the argument was being presented back to front: that if television content becomes reliant on a diet of cheap fast-food programmes, it is not the people's choice that is to blame but precisely the lack of choice.

Having contrived this approach Murdoch was allowed to present himself as a freedom fighter of the underprivileged viewing public by concluding: 'The freeing of broadcasting in this country is very much part of [the] democratic revolution, and an essential step forward into the Information Age.' This statement sits oddly with a man whose democratic revolution only champions those who have enough money for his encrypted subscription, and whose steps towards the 'freeing of broadcasting' have, confusingly, included such broadcasting strangleholds as making a condition of his deal for coverage of the Ryder Cup that even highlights should be unavailable free-to-air, and therefore forbidden to the BBC.

BSB Crushed by Sky's Legal Loophole

In April 1990, BSB finally began direct broadcasting, but the outlook was disastrous. BSB needed to sell 700,000 receivers by the end of the year, and they could not even supply High Street stores with demonstration aerials. Bitter about the unexpected competition from Sky, BSB campaigned vigorously to push the government into bringing medium-powered satellites like Astra under the regulations of the Broadcasting Bill due to become law later that year. Predictably the government was reluctant to close a loophole that had so benefited Murdoch, and prevaricated by saying that Sky used frequencies not allocated by the British government, and a technology which could provide virtually unlimited channels, making the argument of spectrum scarcity irrelevant. This attitude echoed the words of Sky's special public relations office set up in Westminster during the parliamentary debate on the Broadcasting Bill; it was not surprising that the amendment to apply the regulations restricting cross-media ownership to Sky, which would force Murdoch to choose between Sky and his newspapers, was defeated. Meanwhile, BSB was losing £8 million a week.

Murdoch outlives Thatcher

In the face of financial ruin, BSB and Murdoch entered into negotiations and came up with a merger which was in fact illegal. On 29 October 1990 Murdoch met with Margaret Thatcher to apprise her of the situation. He knew he had to get the prime minister on his side before the move was made public, because BSB had no right to share its franchise with Sky. The *New York Times* called it 'a deal that probably has saved the [Murdoch] empire'. The merger was announced a matter of days after the Broadcasting Bill received Royal Assent, to the utter astonishment of the minister responsible for broadcasting, who knew nothing about it. Outrage on the opposition benches, and Labour claims that the whole episode made a nonsense of the new Broadcasting Act, were fuelled by the leak that Thatcher had not only known, but had been personally consulted about the plans, and had told no one. Murdoch now owned 48 per cent of the DBS franchise, which even the Home Secretary acknowledged was not legal. A triumphant Murdoch boasted that he was 'busting the British broadcasting cartel'. Margaret Thatcher was less triumphant: within two weeks of the merger she had been forced to resign.

10   The Thatcher Inheritance

The Broadcasting Act 1990

Although Margaret Thatcher had already been toppled by the time the 1990 Broadcasting Act came into force, issues such as ownership, public service broadcasting and the renewal of Channel 3 franchises were approached from an essentially Thatcherite perspective. However, concessions were brought about by strong pressures from the television broadcasting establishment. The IBA was transformed into the Independent Television Commission (ITC), a body which, in line with Tory policy on the regulation of industry, has less power to intervene in programme policy than its predecessor. Thus it would no longer be responsible for scheduling, a task taken over by the ITV network and would be less involved in the running of the commercial channels. One of the ITC's first duties was to award the Channel 3 franchises which were due for renewal which it did in 1991.

The Daft Auction

In the past the IBA had judged applicants on the basis of their financial credibility, their management proposals and their programme policy. The rules laid down by the Thatcher government envisaged that the ITC would preside over what was in fact an auction. Bids for the franchises would be submitted in sealed envelopes; the highest bidder would win. The idea of allocating franchises, that is, granting access to a scarce public utility on the basis of a gamble, was one of the most extraordinary examples of Thatcherite thinking. Initially, the only criterion was apparently the depth of the applicant's pocket. This extraordinary system was heavily criticised and had to be modified. The result was what one ITV executive described as a 'daft auction' in which some participants – like Scottish television (STV) who guessed that they had little competition, put in a ridiculously low offer, gambled successfully, and won. But where competition was fierce, the sums involved were very large: Carlton Television outbid Thames Television, the London weekday company, by a bid of over £43 million. In some cases the amount put on the table strained the resources of the successful applicants.

Certain categories were excluded from applying: persons (or companies) who were not members of the European Economic Community (EEC), bodies with political connections, religious bodies and advertising agencies. Application forms were long and detailed. They required information about the finances of the applicants, their professional capabilities and their programme policies. An application fee was charged ranging from £80,000 plus VAT for the larger franchises to a mere £7500 for the smallest (the Channel Islands). The bulk of these application fees and enormous bids was paid to the ITC which, acting as a collecting agency, sent them straight to the Treasury. Some previous franchise-holders lost out. Among them were TSW in the South West, TVS in the South and South East and TV AM, the breakfast-time programme company which was judged by the ITC not to have produced programmes of suitable quality. All the old contracts would terminate at the end of 1992. Successful applicants would have to provide services as from 1 January 1993.

It was not as if this cash bid was the end of the financial requirements from the franchise winners. They would be required to make monthly payments for the ten years' duration of their licence. The sum would be in two parts: the cash bid made along with the application plus an amount to be fixed by the ITC. This second figure would vary from licensee to licensee and would depend on their total qualifying revenue (TQR). TQR is an important formula in commercial television in Britain and means the sum of the revenue earned by a licensee from advertising, sponsorship and subscription. (It is open to the licensees to set up subscription services but none has so far done so.) The amount of TQR to be paid for each licence varies from 11 per cent in London to 0 per cent in the smaller companies. The licensees also must pay a fee to the ITC to fund its costs and for the maintenance of the national television archive.

Fortunately, the Thatcherite doctrine of a straightforward auction was circumvented by the ITC which lay down a 'quality threshold'. The definition of this threshold in individual cases would in the nature of things be a subjective one. It was conceivable that two equally high bids would be received but one of the applicants could be held not to have cleared the quality hurdle. The ITC was not under any obligation to justify publicly any decision on quality threshold which was likely to give rise to

objections by an unsuccessful applicant – as has happened with the more
recent applications for the Channel 5 licence, as we shall see.

The Programme Requirements

The requirements demanded of the applicants were at once wide-
ranging and specific. The most debatable is the requirement to provide
'high-quality programmes', a formula which is variously defined. The
ITC describes them as 'programmes which have a special one-off
character' or which show 'marked originality and high production
standards'. Such programmes require 'professionalism and creative
talent'. Some people argue that this is an appeal to élitist tastes; the
commission counters this argument by saying that such programmes
should not be regarded as 'mainly or exclusively of minority appeal'.

In order to ensure diversity the ITC defined nine strands of
programming, which must feature in the programme schedules. They
included the following:

- Drama including single plays, series and serials
- Entertainment including comedy and satire, games and quiz shows,
  chat shows, variety and music
- Sport including coverage of events, magazine and news programmes
- News including newscasts, news magazines and weather forecasts
- Factual programmes including current affairs, e.g. the explanation
  and analysis of events and issues plus more in-depth documentaries.
  There had to be at least 90 minutes of current affairs programmes
  a week dealing with national and international matters.
- Education including adult education and social action
- Religious programmes (at least two hours a week) including the
  broadcasting of acts of worship and programmes examining religious
  issues
- Arts programmes including performances, exhibitions, documentaries reflecting the arts
- Children's programmes (at least ten hours of programmes) aimed
  at children of various ages including entertainment, drama and
  information (the old Reithean trinity of 'inform, educate and
  entertain').

The provision of a 'strong regional service' was regarded by the
Commission as an essential part of the licensee's responsibilities. Regional

services must include regional news programmes reflecting social needs and local activities. The Commission set out a table of the minimum requirements in terms of hours and minutes per week. The contractors in Central Scotland and the North of Scotland must broadcast at least one hour a week on average of programmes in Gaelic together with up to 200 hours a year funded by the Gaelic Television Committee, which is funded in turn by the ITC.

It was an indication of the social concerns of the Commission that the television companies are required to provide subtitling for the deaf. By 1998 at least 50 per cent of the Channel 3 output must be subtitled.

In any year 65 per cent of the programmes broadcast should be produced specially for Channel 3: that is to say only 35 per cent can be bought in from other markets, for example, the US. Moreover 'a proper proportion of programmes must be of European origin.'

Party Political Broadcasts

Another duty laid upon the successful applicants was one of which the broadcasters would gladly be relieved -- that of carrying party political broadcasts (PPBs). This duty applies to the two BBC channels and Channel 3. The number and length of these broadcasts is negotiated (as we have seen) between the BBC and the ITC and the political parties by hard bargaining in which the smaller parties naturally want more airtime and the big ones are reluctant to see it granted. The broadcasters for their part know that the PPBs are highly unpopular with viewers – in fact, a switch off for many. At least they no longer must be carried simultaneously on all channels and can therefore be avoided by those who dislike being offered untrustworthy policies and promises by politicians of all parties, increasingly promoted by the sophisticated techniques of the advertisement makers.

The Successful Applicants

Licences were eventually granted to the following:

- Anglia Television: East of England
- Border Television: the Borders and Isle of Man
- Carlton Television: London weekday
- Central TV: East, West and South Midlands

- Channel TV (CTV): Channel Islands
- Grampian TV: North of Scotland
- Granada TV: North-west England
- HTV: Wales and the West of England
- LWT: London Weekend
- Meridian Broadcasting: South and South-east England
- Scottish Television: Central Scotland
- Tyne Tees TV: North-east England
- Ulster Television: Northern Ireland
- Westcountry Television: South-west England
- Yorkshire TV: Yorkshire
- GMTV: National breakfast-time.

The London franchise was split into two because of the size of the audience and therefore of the amount of advertising revenue available to the licence-holders. LWT broadcasts from 5.15 p.m. on Friday to 6 a.m. on Monday morning and Carlton from 9.25 a.m. on Monday to 5.15 p.m. on Friday. The national breakfast-time franchise runs from 6 a.m. to 9.25 a.m. daily.

The newcomers, Carlton, Meridian, Westcountry and GMTV, replaced the previous licence holders; these were Thames TV, Southern TV and TWW (Television for Wales and the West). Thames continues to be active as an independent programme producer and owner of a valuable television programme library.

Since the franchises were awarded, Tyne Tees TV has merged with Yorkshire TV in a move that prefigured further mergers and take-overs. Granada, for instance, at the time of writing (autumn 1996), was rumoured to have designs on Yorkshire.

The Independents

Hopes had been raised among smaller independent producers by the obligation placed on C3 franchise-holders not to screen more than 75 per cent of programmes produced in-house, that is, in their own studios and with their own production facilities. It soon became clear however that big players, like Granada or Thames, which had lost their franchise, would continue to make programmes and would be in unchallenge-able positions in terms of professional contacts and programme budgets. It also emerged that the executives and consultants of the larger independent production companies were in many cases the same people as had held important positions in the old ITV network. The evidence suggests that even before the franchises had been redistributed 'sweetheart deals' had been struck to guarantee employment should they lose their licences.

The News Service

The news service for Channel 3 is provided by ITN (Independent Television News). ITN was originally a non-profit-making company set up under the 1954 Television Act and jointly owned by the commercial television franchise-holders. It is now an independent company currently owned by a consortium comprising Carlton Communications (36 per cent), the Granada Group (36 per cent), the international newsagency Reuters (18 per cent) and Anglia and Scottish Television (each with 5 per cent). Under the 1990 Broadcasting Act and in line with Thatcherite policies it became a profit-making organisation with commercial contracts with Channels 3 and 4 as well as with a number of radio stations.

For Channel 3, ITN provides three daily bulletins of which the most important is *News at Ten*. This newscast, which was the first half-hour news programme on UK television, claims an average audience of over 6 million as against the BBC's *Nine O'Clock News* of over 5 million. For Channel 4, ITN provides *Channel 4 News* on weekdays and the *Big Breakfast News* for Channel 4's early morning programme. ITN also produces *ITN World News* which is broadcast by satellite to Europe, the United States, Australia and Japan. The cost of the service is calculated at around £60 million per annum.

ITN has enjoyed a monopoly as provider of news for commercial television. With the coming of satellite television Sky News has entered the field and can be expected to become a competitor offering to provide a cheaper news service to the new Channel 5 or any other takers.

The ITV Network

Under the old rules, the IBA (as the regulatory body was then called) as 'the broadcaster' had direct responsibility for the content of the service and approved programme schedules in advance. Under the new dispensation the television companies themselves are responsible for the content and scheduling of programmes; but the ITC has powers to review and comment on their performance and can insist on improvements where it feels that the terms of the act are not being met. It reports to Parliament annually on the performance of the licensees.

Following this change in the role of the ITC the ITV Network Centre came into being to commission and schedule programmes for the network. It is independent of the companies and has its own controllers in the various programme areas – factual programmes, public affairs, drama, children's programmes, entertainment and so on. The controllers commission programmes for the network from the companies or from independent producers. Its schedules are submitted to an ITV Broadcast Board for general approval but the various companies, while they must pay for the programmes provided by the network, have control over their own schedules, subject always to the performance reviews of the ITC.

These reviews are written in the coded language of officialdom but it is clear that the Commission has concerns about the way ITV is going. Thus the 1995 Performance Review, which took account of audience research findings and of reports from the ITC's National Viewer Consultative Councils, noted 'that the balance overall of the schedules [had] shifted noticeably towards more entertainment-led programmes'. The Network Centre had provided less documentary and arts output and 'the less obviously popular programming required by the ITV's public service broadcasting remit, such as education, religion and the arts was often to be found in the margins of the schedules'. There is a hint of regret here for the days when the IBA itself drew up the schedules and insisted that 'less obviously popular' programmes should be put out when there was a reasonable audience for them. It also found that a 'too frequent agenda for factual programmes as well as drama was police work and crime'.

Another concern emerges from the Commission's analysis of the output of individual companies: HTV West, it points out, had a 'high proportion of co-productions with other ITV licensees and with satellite channels'. This, it notes, had the effect of 'diluting regionality and in some cases quality'. The same stricture is applied to LWT co-productions with Granada and Meridian co-productions with Anglia. The comments on the output of Tyne Tees, Westcountry and Yorkshire reflect what appears to be a general anxiety over a failure to reflect regional interests. The division of the United Kingdom into separate franchise areas when ITV came into being was, after all, seen as a way of reflecting local interests, local politics and local society. The Commission's anxiety can only be reinforced by the process whereby the smaller companies are increasingly the targets of takeovers – for reasons which are commercial and financial but have little to do with viewers' needs – by larger companies and by financial organisations, some of them foreign, who are not likely to be interested in reflecting local issues and cultures.

Cable in the 1990s

In the 1990s, cable began to expand in densely populated areas, the only areas that attract the large investment involved in laying and connecting individual households. These developments had been encouraged by the fact that British Telecom is barred from offering broadcast programmes down its lines until the beginning of the next century. Then, in 1996 an important development took place: the merger of Cable and Wireless (which owns the Mercury telephone company) with three UK cable operators – Videotron, Nynex and Bell Cablemedia. The new company – Cable and Wireless Communications – will be the largest provider of telecommunications, information and entertainment services in the UK. This is a direct challenge to British Telecom and also to BSkyB with whom the new company will compete for audiences.

But all is not rosy. Cable companies talk of the number of homes 'passed', but only one in five takes up the multichannel service. The 'churn' factor – the number of people who discontinue their subscriptions after a short time – is high.

The Future of the BBC

As we have seen, the BBC did not escape the influence of the Thatcherite ethos when it came to management and restructuring. The BBC's Chairman in 1986 was Marmaduke Hussey, who had been plucked from a career as an executive at Times Newspapers by the then Home Secretary Douglas Hurd. Hussey recalls how he got a telephone call from Douglas Hurd asking him to be chairman of the BBC although he had almost no experience of broadcasting and little idea what the job involved. Being a known Thatcherite whose wife was a lady-in-waiting to the Queen obviously made him a safe man for the job in the eyes of the government; indeed, he is the only chairman to have served two terms of office in the history of the BBC. (There have been seventeen chairmen altogether.) Other appointments made around the same time were also political place-people. It was Hussey who took the unprecedented step of sacking a director-general, Alasdair Milne, who represented a modified and modernised Reithian tradition. Milne supported the view that primacy should be given to programme making and programme makers. He had come up through current affairs programming and had played an important part in fostering the satirical *That Was The Week That Was*. It is significant that he was replaced by Michael Checkland, an accountant who set in hand far-reaching management changes. He in turn was very soon succeeded by John Birt, the present director-general, who had made his reputation in commercial television as director of programmes at LWT.

Promoted into position by the strong support of Hussey, Birt had the backing to restructure the BBC using the management concepts which were being applied in the National Health Service, education and other previously nationalised industries. In this, he relied heavily on the City management firm of McKinsey and Co. McKinsey, which tends to recruit US business school graduates, has become firmly established as Birt's primary adviser. Under McKinsey and Co.'s influence, Birt speedily introduced a policy of 'producer choice', a measure intended to 'streamline resources and overheads' in the BBC. An internal market was set up and producers were encouraged to shop around for the cheapest resources either in-house or outside. This policy has its parallel in the shopping around for resources in the NHS.

The market policy has been accompanied by the fragmentation and casualisation of the work-force on the one side and on the other the greatly increased centralisation of power in the hands of the controllers of BBC1 and BBC2. Those who have to deal with the BBC under the new system complain of bureaucracy and difficulty in obtaining programme decisions. The streamlining process has meant the disbanding of centres of professional skill – for example, the film department – and the decline in technical and journalistic training for which the BBC had a high reputation.

With uncertainty of employment, the increased centralisation of power and the secrecy of management and governors, a work environment of dictatorship and fear is created. In the broadcasting industry, management dictatorship spreads to become editorial dictatorship, a phenomenon that directly affects the viewers who fund the BBC.

The Renewal of the BBC's Charter

These changes took place at a time when the BBC was preparing for a renewal of its Charter. In what was clearly intended as a demonstration of the extent to which it had absorbed the new ethos, the BBC in 1992 published an expensively glossy brochure entitled *Extending Choice*. In it the BBC presented a case for the 'core services' to continue to be funded by the licence fee, but allowed that 'the BBC will continue energetically to explore additional revenue streams' and 'to pursue . . . supplementary funding for secondary distribution services with limited access'. These would include revenue from sales of the BBC World Service Television programmes and profits from BBC Enterprises' sales (both now incorporated into BBC Worldwide Ltd, the BBC's 'commercial arm'), profits from subscription television, co-production and publishing businesses and sponsorship of public arts and sporting events. Presenting a dynamic commercial profile while still claiming to be a public service is a difficult balancing act. While the BBC was keen to point out that these supplementary income streams would not 'invalidate the need for the licence fee', critics felt that this 'mixed funding' transmogrified the BBC into a business whereby cost-cutting methods turned what was a 'centre for broadcasting excellence' into a conveyor belt of programmes as commodities.

The renewal of the Charter – which will run until 2006 – was made more probable by the BBC's adoption of Thatcherite management methods, as well as a change in tone by the new Conservative Prime Minister John Major. At the end of the Gulf War he went out of his way in the Commons to praise the BBC's coverage. This had been noticeably safe and was careful not to overstep the rigid restrictions placed on reporting by the military authorities in the Gulf, who, with their talk of super-accurate weapons, contrived to make their operations look and sound like a video game. (It is only recently that the same US military spokesmen who boasted of the technical efficiency of these rockets and bombs have admitted that their version was far from the truth. The anti-ballistic missiles sent to protect Israel from rocket attacks by Iraq were in fact a failure, not the immense success that was proclaimed at the time.)

The Dangers to the BBC

The shape of the BBC in the 1990s has been the subject of much anxious comment. In 1992 Sir David Attenborough, a distinguished programme maker who as a senior BBC executive was head of BBC 2, said 'The BBC is being gravely eroded, the morale of its staff seriously damaged, and the very things that gave it its unique stature and strength destroyed.'

Michael Grade, the head of Channel 4, in his McTaggart Lecture at the Edinburgh Television Festival in 1992 spoke for many when he said that he believed the BBC governors had 'adopted a policy of political appeasement. They have half embraced the free market but in doing so have set the BBC on a course leading to terminal decline.' It was an apparent paradox that when the BBC was under attack by Thatcher it was frequently defended (and continues to be so) by spokesmen for the ITV companies. Their favourite line of argument is that the BBC should be left as it is as a licence-funded public service organisation because, by its standards and range of programming, it provides an example for the ITV companies which might otherwise give in to purely commercial considerations. They are no doubt sincere in thus defending the public service ethos against strong commercial pressures; a cynic might add however that the last thing the ITV network wishes to see is a commercialised BBC (with its high standards of programming) competing for advertising revenue. The signs are that the advertising cake is not indefinitely large. Channel 5 and satellite broadcasting are already competing for their share and digital broadcasting may soon be doing so. Margaret Thatcher may have left office at the beginning of the decade but the BBC continues down the commercial slope. In October 1995, the BBC applied for £70 million from the Millennium Commission causing even a Conservative MP to describe the corporation's 'quest for commercialism' as 'chutzpah'.

For those who wish to see the principles of public service broadcasting survive, the news that Sir Christopher Bland was appointed chairman of the BBC in 1996 can only be bad. Bland, a one-time member of the Conservative think-tank the Bow Group, was chairman of LWT and deputy chairman of Nynex, the American cable operator, positions which made him more than £9 million and gave him an assured position at the top of the social pile. With a suitably horsey analogy Bland supports mixed funding: 'You've been given one really good horse in the licence fee. You can justify it if you ride it well and carefully. The other sources can provide the saddle, the bridle, but it's not the same as having two horses.' He has however stated that increasing the licence fee (£1.75 billion in 1995) is 'one of the major short-term issues for the BBC'. Bland's arrival as chairman could make the current director-general John Birt's position more comfortable. Ever since controversy raged about the secret and unorthodox nature of Birt's appointment, Birt has been viewed as a pawn of the governors and therefore of government, and his policies have been criticised as having little creative vision. Most of the decline of morale within the corporation has been laid at his door.

11 Digital Television

The last decade of the twentieth century has seen great changes in telecommunications. These changes are taking place in the field of technology and, as a consequence, in the aims and organisation of the television industry itself.

The Digital Revolution

The technological developments are those described in Chapter 1: digitisation of the television signals leads to a huge increase in the number of channels available, both terrestrial and satellite, the introduction of interactive television, the convergence of various media (e.g. broadcasting, publishing, computers), all of which form a multimedia information superhighway. Digitisation has also facilitated the development of high-definition wide-screen television. These developments are seen by powerful economic interests as providing opportunities for large profits in an expanding market in which there will be opportunities for those who create the content, those who package it (channel owners and publishers) and those who distribute it (operators using cable, satellite, terrestrial and telecom delivery systems).

New Problems and New Hardware

The coming of digital television presents problems for all the parties concerned: the broadcasters, the viewers and the government.

For the broadcasters the question is: Where are the programmes to come from to fill the channels? This problem they hope to resolve in part by the acquisition of film libraries and archival material including backlogs of sitcoms, series and serials; but there is no doubt that economic pressures will mean that cheap television programmes – chatshows and quizzes – will proliferate. It is an observed phenomenon that in television more (in terms of channels) means not diversity but more of the same.

Where the viewers are concerned they will have to acquire a set-top box to receive the standard digital terrestrial TV (DTTV) channels available for BBC1, BBC2, ITV, Channel 4 and Channel 5. Digital satellite television (DSTV) and digital cable television (DCTV) will also have to be decoded although, alarmingly, no compatible system has been legislated for in the UK, a lack that could mean the viewer will need more than one set-top box. Viewers may have to choose one of these three delivery systems if they decide to buy the new television hardware.

The government of the day will face a problem connected with the choice of a date for the switch-over from analogue to digital television. If the analogue system is switched off, viewers who have not bought a set-top decoder box or a new digital television set to enable them to receive the digital signal will find their TV sets useless. Potential investors in digital are keen to see a definite date for a switch-over which would stimulate (that is, force) the sale of digital hardware and services. A change-over taking place over a period of time may soften the financial blow for viewers but would deter positive investment and definite planning for DTTV. The government has so far procrastinated (any decision is obviously seen to be a potential vote-loser), saying it will review the situation after five years or when DTTV reaches 50 per cent of households. Whenever digital bites, the government will automatically be held responsible for forcing viewers to pay for the set-top boxes necessary to receive the new digital broadcasting. Clearly, many viewers will not be able to afford either the decoders, (they are expected to cost approximately £500) or the extremely expensive digital sets (currently estimated at around £1000). A large number of people will find that television has been priced out of their reach although no doubt prices will fall over time. As with the transition from a 405-line to a 625-line system, and from black-and-white to colour transmission, a considerable number of viewers in a society where poverty is increasing will not be able to update their equipment.

Government ministers and broadcasters who need to persuade viewers that a digital system is desirable point out that in comparison with digital broadcasting the analogue system will appear as anachronistic and unappealing as black-and-white sets became once colour television was introduced. This is a disingenuous argument. In the first place, owners of black-and-white sets were able to continue receiving programmes as usual and had the power to choose when they invested in colour reception themselves. Secondly, television licence fees increased more for operators of colour sets than for those with black and white. The change-over was viewer-led. This will not be the case with digital broadcasting.

New Prices for Programming

The changes limiting those who cannot afford to spend any more of their budget on television viewing will not stop at the new hardware necessary. The digital channels available on satellite will carry an increasing number of pay-per-view sporting events and other 'exclusives' which will be encrypted and available only to subscribers. Many of these services will be aimed at an important section of the viewing public – males in the top economic categories of AB and C1 – whom the advertisers wish to attract because they are the people with spending power, many of whom still control the domestic purse-strings. Television companies will continue to spend their money buying up film rights and above all sports rights, 'golden oldies' and other proven successes for themed subscription channels, and will also be racing to develop the new broadcast services such as the widely hyped interactive television – home shopping, home banking, video on demand (VOD) and television access to the internet – to woo the largest slice of society with the largest slice of disposable income. It is hard to see how those who cannot afford this exciting new television world will not become second-class viewers. Any interactive debate will be barred to them. In 1996 approximately five million households in Britain were still without a phone. How many households will be without a modem, a set-top box, and the cash for the necessary subscriptions?

Provision for Digital Television in the UK

The 1996 Broadcasting Act laid down regulations for the launch of digital terrestrial TV in the UK over the next ten to fifteen years, providing for the licensing of an anticipated eighteen digital channels on six multiplexes. 'Multiplexes' are clusters of at least three TV channels carried on a single digital frequency. Under the proposals, broadcasters and other media companies will be able to bid for licences as 'multiplex providers', offering a selection of digital programming. The existing ITV companies such as Carlton, Yorkshire, Tyne Tees, LWT and Granada, will be guaranteed half a multiplex each, and will be able to bid for additional capacity subject to a ceiling of 15 per cent of the total television audience. In return, they must 'simulcast' at least 80 per cent of the existing ITV analogue schedule. The BBC has been awarded an entire multiplex. The proposals, when first published in a White Paper in December 1995, appeared to satisfy all the big players in the television industry. The chairman of the ITV Association said, 'The Government has listened to the industry and sought to accommodate our views.' The director of programming at BSkyB said, 'We see this as an endorsement of multichannel choice, of pay-TV and digital TV. It opens the door to Sky to play the role of a multi-service provider.'

Digital Satellite Television – DSTV

In satellite broadcasting the race to provide digital services is well under way. In April 1995, Eutelsat, one of the world's biggest satellite operators, started test transmissions from the new satellite Hot Bird 1. This marked the introduction of digital satellite broadcasting to Europe. In September 1996, Eutelsat launched Hot Bird 2, with Hot Bird 3 following in February 1997. SES – *Société Européenne des Satellites* – the private Luxemburg-based owner of the Astra system used by BSkyB, launched the all-digital Astra 1E in autumn 1995, 1F in spring 1996 and plans to launch 1G in 1997.

The first to launch DSTV in Europe was Telepiù in Italy in January 1996 with the backing of the German group Kirch and Nethold, which combines Swiss and South African interests and illustrates the international nature of the companies and finance involved. In the spring of 1996 the French Canal Plus launched Canal Satellite Numérique (*numérique* means digital) offering ten theme channels including sports and travel together with a pay-per-view movie channel. In the summer of 1996 the Kirch group in Germany launched DF1 (Digital Fernsehen 1) offering a twenty-channel package.

It would clearly be in the interest of the viewers if all digital signals were available to them whether they came from BSkyB, for example, from the BBC's future digital services, or from the cable companies. All digital services will require a decoder unit, which will eventually be incorporated inside every television. The problem in the UK is that BSkyB is the first to develop the technology, which means that it could block its competitors. The technology it has in place includes an encryption, decoding and billing system which in addition administers the list of their subscribers and bills them for the services they use. Digital will not work without this technology, or a similar one, to unscramble the signal.

Sky's dominant position on the new digital Astra satellites gives it approximately 150 to 200 digital channels, together with massive data capacity. BSkyB say they are ready to begin transmitting in 1997, although their profits for analogue satellite subscription are so high that introducing DSTV, which would force consumers to buy new hardware, might have the adverse effect of slowing profits down. It is from a confidently dominant position that BSkyB's director of programmes has expressed interest in bidding for digital terrestrial licences as well.

The BBC in the Digital Age

While BSkyB grows apace the BBC has been slower in securing a place on the digital platform. The cost of the technology and the fact that the government was slow to allocate this extra digital capacity has prevented the corporation from so far becoming a digital innovator. Financial constraints too have hindered the BBC. DTTV will require the BBC to install new transmitters and re-equip generally, which would mean a large capital outlay at a time when the BBC faces financial insecurity. One solution favoured by the government was that the BBC should privatise its transmission services; the BBC resisted this but finally had to give in. NTL (National Transmission Ltd), the transmission company formerly owned by the Independent Broadcast Authority which oversees ITV transmission, bid for the BBC's transmitter network in 1996. The success of this bid would result in a near-monopoly on transmission services in the UK.

The cost of introducing digital television is adduced as one of the main reasons for the programme of 'reforms' that Birt has carried through. The problem is that the revenue from the licence fee is limited and no government is likely to wish to increase this unpopular direct tax – so where and how is the BBC to obtain the necessary funds? The answer lies in increasing commercialisation. In a publication brought out in May 1996 entitled *Extending Choice in the Digital Age* , the BBC outlined its intention to

> increase the financial contribution from our commercial activities . . . For those viewers who want to pay for even greater choice . . . BBC Worldwide Ltd . . . will include themed subscription channels, a full

range of multimedia and online products and – eventually –
programmes which can be ordered truly on-demand.

Viewers who 'want to pay' or who, more accurately, can afford to pay
extra will have access to these services by opening a subscription account
which pays for the decoding of these encrypted services.

This presents the danger that 'free-to-air' television will become the
poor relation to the subscription channels, and that a two-tier broadcasting
system will develop. The money to place the BBC in the digital arena
has to come from somewhere. The BBC has insisted that money could
be found by a further push towards increased efficiency, usually a
euphemism for loss of jobs and a substantial cut in the production budget.
Despite this announcement, it came as no surpirse that John Birt pled
the case for a substantial increase in the licence fee in his lecture at the
Edinburgh Television Festival in August 1996. The productions that
are funded in the future will be highly publicised flagships which will
almost certainly need to claw back some of their costs from some form
of extra subscription charges. Any introduction of subscription by the
BBC will end the viewers' automatic right to access because each
programme made will have its fate decided by a BBC executive who
will rule whether any part (and which part) or all constitutes
'supplementary programming'. These decisions will be heavily influenced
by the need to make subscription supplementary programmes attractive
enough for people to want to spend more money on their viewing of
BBC output, over and above the television licence. The BBC would
be risking the success of their efforts to make money from subscription
if they broadcast too much prime programming on the basic 'free-to-
air' channels, presenting themselves with the same competition they now
face externally from the commercial channels. It is a very schizophrenic
scheme.

The BBC have indicated that extra content to fuel the new channels
will come from increased sports coverage – coverage, that is, that has
not already been bought by the larger purse of BSkyB – a 24-hour news
operation, more coverage of arts festivals such as the Prom concerts and
'gavel-to-gavel' footage of party conferences and key Commons debates.
The BBC have given VE Day as an example of an event that would
have had increased television coverage with digital technology. With
a single multiplex, the BBC would have been able to show VE Day
events at length and at one and the same time from different parts of
the UK. There has been no promise of extra productions being financed.

The Digital Platform

To become a digital player the BBC must compete not only with other content providers, but with the companies that are forging ahead with the new digital technology. The government has attempted to encourage development of digital services by offering licences free for the first twelve years to possible digital providers with an automatic extension after this, subject to satisfactory performance. Licences will be awarded by the ITC on the basis of how quickly bidders propose to start digital coverage and on programming quality. These provisions slowly became incorporated into state legislature when the 1996 Broadcast Bill was passed but there is a very real possibility that government regulations have missed the boat, failing to manage the digital potential in much the same way as they failed to harness the satellite market in the 1980s.

In the event Murdoch has almost certainly gained a powerful potential monopoly by the government's inability to impose regulation of a common digital platform and some controlled form of profit-sharing. Sky's digital decoders will be satellite specific: they will not decode the digital signals of the terrestrial broadcasters or the cable companies when they come on-stream. This lack of provision of a common platform for digital television in the UK is a cause for much concern and places the future of British DTTV in jeopardy.

In September 1995, the ITV company Yorkshire–Tyne Tees held informal talks with French satellite broadcaster Canal Plus about developing a digital service to compete with Rupert Murdoch's pay-TV system, thus avoiding Murdoch control. This would mean several different set-top boxes would be necessary, which, from the viewer's point of view, would be a nightmare. It would be a rare household that would be prepared to buy more than one box. As the market for broadcast equipment experienced with the launch of satellite dishes, the first new technology on the market nearly always wins the race, and subsequently controls the medium. With BSkyB set to launch the first digital platform in Britain every other UK broadcaster could be bound to Murdoch's technology, and follow in the old BSB's footsteps by having to bow to Murdoch control and speed of innovation. Despite the ITC announcing in the spring of 1996 that it was preparing a code of practice on the technology to cover the conformity of terrestrial, satellite and cable digital broadcasting technology nothing concrete had been implemented at the time of writing (autumn 1996).

The implications of such a monopoly for the viewer are centred around freedom of information, choice and access. For all television companies with their individual investment in digital technology the issue of a standardised decoding system is a crucial financial one. Kirch with its Telepiù partner Nethold developed the conditional access system D-Box. Canal Plus and Bertelsmann are using MediaBox. Neither of these are compatible with each other or the system developed by BSkyB. The European Parliament is well ahead of the British government in voting for open access to conditional access systems, for published tariffs applicable equally to all, and for an arbitration mechanism and legal recourse to the EU judicial system for any alleged transgression by the gatekeepers of digital TV. The industry commissioner for the European Commission, Martin Bangeman, called Europe's key media companies to a meeting as early as June 1995 to plan for a common digital interface. Although the EC is optimistic that they have the industry's support for a common standard whatever decoder is chosen, the single system will have an enormous impact on the power bases of these companies. This has wider implications than the control of broadcasting: digital technology is the platform for the convergence of broadcasting, publishing, computers and telecommunications. For this reason it is essential that there are many diverse and equally powerful gatekeepers of the future who will allow for the widest choice and access of every electronic communication, information and entertainment.

12 Convergence

The new millennium will see the results of the great changes in television broadcasting, changes which are already under way. They are being brought about by developments which are leading to the convergence of three main technologies – television, telephony and computing – all of whom are competing for the biggest slice of the broadcasting market. These technologies include digital terrestrial broadcasting, digital satellite transmissions, cable distribution systems, video-on-demand (VOD), electronic publishing, the development of CD-Roms, the expansion of the Internet and the exploitation of film archives. It is a future in which television sets, some predict, will become single multimedia terminals – for those who can afford the equipment. It is a development foreshadowed by experiments in the UK using British Telecom lines and set-top boxes which allow customers to carry out banking transactions and home shopping. These changes in the transmission, distribution and storage of television signals and programming have been accompanied by a corresponding upheaval in the ownership and control of the media. These are world-wide phenomena. The market-place for the television industry has become a global one.

The Struggle for Control

By the mid-1990s it was already evident that a struggle was taking place between financial giants for control of the lucrative media market of which television – the world-wide mass medium – was the most important part. The big players in this competition, many of whom are interconnected, were engaged in a bewildering array of shifting alliances and rivalries. The struggle to dominate the delivery and content of the converging media on a global scale has been carried out on three levels.

Takeovers Within the UK

In the UK, for example, the first area where media corporations felt the need to expand was in the domestic market. The pressure was for a change in the rules which limited the ownership of the television companies which make up the ITV network. The argument advanced was that the ITV companies which had been set up to serve regional and local interests were too small, too under-financed and under-resourced to compete in an international market with competitors like the US film and television giant, Time-Warner. There was talk in the Conservative press of the 'glittering job-creating prizes to be won' which 'British firms must be freed to go out and seize'.

One obstacle in the way of such a concentration of money and power lay in the 1990 Television Act which ruled that the ITV companies could hold only one licence. But pressure from the interested parties led to an amendment to the Act passed by the Conservative government in 1993 which allowed ITV companies to own two franchises, with shares of up to 20 per cent in a third. This prompted a round of takeovers that left commercial terrestrial television in the UK dominated by three major powers – MAI (Mills and Allen International), United News & Media, Carlton and Granada.

MAI, owned by the Labour peer Lord Hollick, already owned the south of England franchise-holder, Meridian. To this it added Anglia and 15 per cent of Yorkshire as well as gaining a stake in the new Channel 5. In 1996, MAI engineered a £3 billion merger with United News & Media, the owners of (amongst others) the *Daily Express* and *Sunday Express*. United News & Media has since acquired almost 20 per cent of HTV.

This is a process that is set to go further. In Scotland, STV has acquired Caledonian Newspapers, publishers of the important *Glasgow Herald*, and is likely to aim at taking over Grampian and Border Television. STV's extension into newspaper ownership led it to request a scrutiny of its operations by the ITC, which is required under the 1996 Act to ensure that takeovers do not restrict diversity of information or restrict market forces. The ITC found that it was not against the public interest. Other ITV companies followed suit. Granada, despite fierce resistance from LWT, took over the London weekend television franchise and Carlton merged with Central. Now, Carlton and Granada together own 36 per cent of ITN. In February 1996, Granada, flushed with the success of its takeover of the Forte empire, bought 14 per cent of Yorkshire Television. This brought its holdings to 24 per cent, 4 per cent over the legal allowance. Granada employed an ingenious phrase here, making a statement that it was 'warehousing' the illegal extra 4 per cent.

The question is whether as the ITV companies become bigger, richer, more powerful – and fewer – they will necessarily produce better programmes or adequately serve the needs of local and regional audiences. It is noticeable that in its 1996 annual report on the output of the network since the process of amalgamation and take-overs began, the ITC remarked on the decrease in regional programming and the neglect of local issues.

The BBC has not remained untouched by this process. Towards the end of 1996, the BBC announced further moves to maximise profits in its aim to secure a powerful global position. The technical operations involved in programme-making – studios, editing suites, camera units, etc. – were separated from the initial creative processes and planning, the former being managed by BBC Resources. Resources earns an income of over £700 million a year providing technical facilities of all kinds not only for the BBC's producers (who operate within an internal market) but also for independent producers. The next logical step would be to hive Resources off into a separate, privately owned company. The sale and the freedom the newly created company would have from the financial restrictions imposed on a publicly owned utility which prevent it from borrowing or investing capital would raise much needed funds to help finance the costly development of digitisation. Hybrid ventures – part public, part privatised – such as the NHS, have been cited by BBC managers and Conservative economists as success stories despite the well-documented conflicts imposed by such mixed funding. Each new move towards commercialisation will make justifying the levy of the licence fee, let alone the proposed increase to this tax, more difficult.

Cross-media Ownership and the 1996 Broadcast Bill

In the UK, recent legislation which purported to address the issue of cross-media ownership has left many politically confused. Traditionally, many of the electorate would have looked to Labour to protect the interests of the work-force against huge conglomerates who hold unions in an increasingly dependent position and to guard against the opportunity these media empires have to build up a monopolistic editorial control that spreads across the different media. However, as the Broadcast Bill went through Parliament the voices supporting closer restrictions on cross-media ownership appeared to belong to the Conservatives.

It is an ironic example of the power cross-media ownership has allowed the media moguls of the 1990s that informs Labour's reluctance to support legislation that will limit, amongst others, Murdoch's control of the British media. Fears that Murdoch still has the power to do to Blair what he did to Kinnock seems to be behind Labour's move to draft an amendment to the Bill proposing the jettisoning of the government's limit on the newspaper market share above which a group may not control a Channel 3 franchise. The amendment was defeated, as was a counter-amendment tabled by 73 Labour backbenchers seeking to reduce this limit to 10 per cent. The limit of the newpaper market share set by the Conservatives was fixed at 20 per cent thereby excluding Murdoch and the traditionally pro-Labour Mirror group from owning a commercial terrestrial television franchise.

Another amendment, that would effectively have supported the practice of 'warehousing' holdings in newpapers and television companies that take conglomerates over the legal limit by allowing them a year to dispose of the surplus was supported by Labour. It was left to a spokesperson of the government to point out that it was ' perfectly straightforward under competition law' for a company to have to sell one asset to acquire another. The time limit that companies have to sell off any excess holdings under the 1996 Broadcast Bill was set at three months. It is by no means certain that the relevant regulatory bodies such as the Monopolies and Mergers Commission or the ITC have sufficient power to implement these legal limits effectively.

The 1996 Broadcasting Act contained a further move to relax cross-media regulations. Under this new law a company was allowed to own as many licences as it could acquire provided it did not control more than 15 per cent of the total viewing audience. These measures however did not address the thornier issues of the implications of cross-media ownership within the digital media world. As the boundaries between traditional broadcasting, print-based media, information technology and telecommunications become blurred, regulations that not only guarantee universal access but also that prevent the emergence of monopolies that will restrict or manipulate the flow of information have become imperative. Effective proposals to establish and implement such regulations have been absent from both political parties' policy statements.

International Takeovers

On an international level a struggle for supremacy in the European and global communications industry involves large and complex organisations with interests that reach across national frontiers. Dominating this struggle and building formidable media empires have been:

- In France: Havas, a news agency, with interests in newspaper and book publishing, in Canal Plus (the French commercial television channel), in cable channels in France, and in pay-per-view in Spain, Belgium, Germany and Poland. It also has a stake in Capital Radio.
- In Luxemburg: CLT (Compagnie Luxembourgeoise de Télédiffusion) which runs the most popular television channel in Germany and owns more than twenty television and radio stations over northern Europe. In the UK, it has interests in Channel 5, in Talk Radio and Country 1035 in London and owns 80 per cent of the Irish pop station Atlantic 252 with its wide UK coverage. Havas is the largest shareholder in CLT.
- In Germany: Bertelsmann, a global communications organisation with large interests in books, magazines and newspaper publishing in Europe and the United States and owner of 14 per cent of the world music industry. It has recently merged its broadcasting interests with CLT.
- Also in Germany: Leo Kirch, Bertelsmann's greatest rival, has large interests in television and newspapers including Germany's biggest tabloids. He also owns a huge film library and controls Sat 1, the second largest commercial channel in Germany. In 1995 he acquired the television rights for the 2002 and 2006 football World Cups.
- In Italy: Silvio Berlusconi, the newspaper magnate and ex-prime minister, through his media group Fininvest, owns three television channels which he shamelessly used to secure his election and to urge viewers to support the right-of-centre political parties: his own Forza Italia and the Freedom Alliance. He also has television interests in Spain. At one time he expressed interest in Channel 5 in the UK but then withdrew.

The Inward Investors

In Britain, Murdoch's BSkyB, which is technically not UK-based, has established a controlling position in satellite and pay-per-view television in Britain; but the most concentrated overseas takeovers have affected cable television. Many of the ventures funded by foreign interests are examples of that 'inward investment' which was one of the developments encouraged by and boasted of by the Major government.

It was in line with this policy that the major American cable and telecommunications companies were given a strong incentive to invest in 'cabling up' Britain in the form of a regulation which denies British Telecom (BT) the right to send broadcast entertainment down its lines. An example is provided by Nynex, a big American company which has shares in Viacom which in turn owns the satellite channels MTV and Nickleodeon, and which controls the film production company Paramount. Nynex currently owns 18 franchises throughout the UK while Telewest (a joint venture between Tele-Communications Inc. and US West) has 24 franchises. Both companies made a deal with BSkyB protecting their reciprocal interests with detailed contracts including 'no-compete' clauses and agreements over retail price management. This effectively sewed up half the UK cable market thus making entry for any new company extremely difficult.

Competition for Content

From the mid-1990s onward, it was clear that the last years of the century would see a rapid increase in the number of television channels available to the viewing public. In 1996 the telephone company AT&T were advertising the availability in the US of their 175 digital satellite channels. What was less clear was where the programmes were to come from to satisfy the demand from a multipicity of outlets given over to round-the-clock transmission. One obvious answer was sport, which became the most sought-after brand of televison programming. It was not surprising, therefore, that Murdoch's BSkyB made the satellite broadcasting of sport the keystone of its programme policy. In pursuit of this policy it struck a £670 million four-year deal with UK football's Premier League for live coverage of matches. It thus outbid the MAI group which had offered £1.6 billion for a 10-year contract and the Carlton-Mirror Group which offered £650 million over four years. The BBC, meantime, although outclassed by Murdoch in terms of cash, also entered the market, outbidding ITV for soccer highlights for £73 million safeguarding their *Match of the Day* which had for years been the Corporation's flagship sports programme. (However, it lost Formula One motor racing and the FA cup to ITV.)

This large investment on Murdoch's part aroused suspicion that he would proceed at some point to pay-per-view for Premier League soccer.

Exclusive rights to sporting events are very attractive to the broadcaster wishing to persuade viewers to pay for programmes at the point of delivery mainly because sports coverage is so much more valuable 'live' than recorded for deferred transmission. Highlights of a cup final match when everyone knows the outcome are not nearly so compelling and lose much of the shared mass cultural appeal. The largest section of viewers for these events is made up of young, relatively affluent males who could afford to pay-per-view to see either individual matches or to take out a season ticket for coverage of their favourite club. Nor would pay-per-view be limited to football. BSkyB used the Tyson versus Bruno boxing match in February 1996 as a test-run for pay-per-view and took more than £5 million. It became clear that charging audiences for viewing particular transmissions was a lucrative vein ripe for exploitation.

Characteristically in Britain it was the threat of BSkyB buying up exclusive rights to major sporting events, and in some cases creating its own that, in the spring of 1996, caused the House of Lords to overrule the government and vote to keep eight sporting events, such as Wimbledon, the FA Cup and the Derby available to terrestrial television and therefore free-to-air. This averted the danger of any BSkyB deal for exclusive rights to these 'national treasures'. It is interesting to note that the government, represented by National Heritage Minister Virginia Bottomley, was not moved to oppose Murdoch and his shopping spree for sports in the UK.

The competition for content also explains the race of every major broadcaster in Europe to secure rights to the huge film libraries in Hollywood, in addition to music rights, and to make links with broadcasters who have archival material in the shape of old sitcoms and serials, nature programmes and documentaries. The various rights come under the heading 'intellectual property'.

Convergence, Confusion and Control

The desire to buy up content also explains the moves made by the telecommunications and computer software industries to link with broadcasters. Broadcasters like the BBC, rich in programming but lacking in digital technical developments, will be under increasing pressure to trade with those conglomerates who control the digital delivery systems in order for their programmes to be carried. Telecommunications companies in particular possess a rich cable network of enormous interest to broadcasters. In the UK, many talks and unofficial deals are being struck with BT while the regulation that bars entertainment from being carried down their lines is in force. The Labour Party has promised to end this regulation earlier than the official deadline of 2001 provided in return that BT connect schools to the Internet.

The deal between Murdoch's News Corp and MCI, the US telecommunications giant in which BT has a 20 per cent stake, is an example of how the convergence of these technologies could lead to all information and entertainment becoming controlled by one source. Telephone companies are keen to join content providers as they are only too aware that, while the interactive infrastructure provided by their telephone networks are vital delivery systems, if they have no investment in content their assets are empty. MCI, which has already invested in data and video communications, electronic mail and network management, bought approximately $1 billion of preferred stock in News Corp, with an option to acquire an additional $1 billion, giving Murdoch an extra $2 billion with which to further his development and control of digital broadcasting in the UK. Here we see how entertainment, broadcasting and telephony have been brought together under one corporate roof. Other alliances which bring the different technologies together include the merger of Disney, which bought the US television network ABC, with AT&T, the largest long-distance operator in the US, thus converging films, television, theme parks and telephony. One of the richest men in the world, wonder boy Bill Gates has linked his Microsoft empire with DreamWorks, a huge film, television and multimedia joint venture created by another erstwhile wunderkind, film mogul Steven Spielberg, the former Disney chief Jeffrey Katzenberg and David Geffen, the music impresario. Time-Warner have interests in electronic publishing, magazines, films, television and cable. Pearson Mindscape, the British conglomerate, which has won the franchise for Channel 5 in the UK, has shares in publishing, theme parks, television and broadcasting.

Significantly, these multimedia giants are predominantly American (Murdoch became an American citizen to be able to buy up an American television network) and the bulk of the intellectual property rights are American-owned. Britain has few resources with which to compete except in the pop music industry and, to a more limited extent, in the provision of archival programmes, a resource which the BBC will no doubt exploit as it ventures further into the market-place.

Niche Television

One important development has been the growth of 'niche' television in which Sky Sport is a pioneer and of which the Sci-Fi channel, which came on air in 1995, is another example. It seems inevitable that the multiplication of channels must lead to increasing specialisation in terms of programmes and in terms of the audience addressed. This trend was already established in the mid-1990s with the Playboy channel delivering soft porn and more serious interests being catered for by the European News channel and the Parliamentary channel, all available on cable. An important player in these developments has been Flexitech, a cable company based in the UK but controlled by the American company Telecommunications Inc. (TCI). It has links with the BBC in the UK Gold Channel.

One form of niche television is exemplified by the activities of Pearsons, the media, publishing and leisure company. In 1991 it bought Thames, which used to share the London ITV franchise but, on losing out to Carlton, became an independent production company. Thames's attraction for Pearsons is in the business of marketing programmes. To this end it has bought up what are called 'concept rights', programme formats which can then be produced in different countries. This development is ominously known as 'template television' and seems likely to prove the truth of the old adage that in television 'more' means 'more of the same'.

Convergence and Regulation

The convergence of technologies has brought with it problems of regulation − regulation in the sense of the location of facilites and in the sense of the control of quality and content.

The first question is: Who is to regulate the merging systems given that computers, telecommunications systems and broadcasting delivery systems will all be involved? In 1995 the ITC severely criticised the government over its proposal to give the telephone regulator Oftel more power over pay-per-view and digital television. In the same year, in a green paper setting out proposals for digital television, the government said that 'broadcasters should be licensed under the Telecommunications Act; after consultation on the licence conditions with the ITC and other interested parties, and subsequently regulated by Oftel, working closely with the ITC'. One of the ITC's main demands has been that all providers of information, not just television companies, must be licensed by the ITC. Michael Grade (controller of Channel 4) pointed out that much valuable revenue could be created were the telecommunications companies to have some of their enormous profits taxed and levied in a similar way as those of the broadcasting companies which are subject to a levy and tax. If this income were hypothecated – that is, earmarked for a specific purpose, in this case investment back into the broadcasting industry – British television, he argued, would have a much needed injection of capital with which to develop digital services and fund productions. Both the two regulators and their respective government departments – Trade and Industry for Oftel and National Heritage for the ITC – have given the impression of being more divisively partisan than collaborative and a political struggle for control over earth-based and satellite networks seems likely.

There is a second and more difficult problem: how can the regulators, with over 500 channels and more than three million pages of information, entertainment and advertising on the Internet to patrol, in any practical sense hope to apply a code of standards concerning 'good taste and decency' and impartiality which were signed up to by the BBC and the ITV network companies and formed the ground rules of public service broadcasting?

The difficulties are more complicated than those of mere administration. In the last thirty years in Western society the old solid consensus has crumbled. In the UK the common front of the monarchy, the political parties, the Church, the broadsheets, can no longer be taken for granted. Too many changes have taken place in what is now a multi-ethnic society in which old deferences have been eroded and replaced by new attitudes. Some spring from the assertion of women's rights, the rights of the gay community and changing perceptions of sex and sexuality, others from the emergence of green politics and the decline of the Old Left. All these inform ways of thinking and of expression which do not find a place in the consensus. Some of the most profound changes were initiated by Thatcherite economic and social policies which have resulted in the creation of a permanent core group of unemployed and insecure, and a deep feeling of alienation among those adversely affected by poverty, neglect and deprivation. These are changes which have affected even white-collar workers who once felt themselves secure. In this climate of social disintegration it is not surprising that old moral certainties and judgements on 'taste' should be increasingly difficult to apply.

New Gatekeepers

We have discussed the concept of gatekeeping in the context of editorial control of programmes. But gatekeping has taken on a new meaning with the increase in cross-media ownership and above all in the control over access to the digital transmission platforms. An obvious result is provided by the powerful position Murdoch established by putting out tenders for the design and manufacture of the set-top equipment for the reception of BSkyB's encrypted digital television signals in the UK. Viewers will be forced to buy a second digital decoding system for the terrestrial channels. Having thus established a lead in the development of the digital services of the BBC and ITV channels, Murdoch will be in the powerful position of gatekeeper controlling the digital gateway. The international consortia, with their cross-media ownership of which he is the head, will have the power to shape public opinion and cultural identities and to offer, instead of a diversity of programmes 'template television'.

The danger is that discussion, debate and opinion – in short, the public space – will become homogenised and sanitised and thus a more effective 'opium of the people' than has ever been known. Even traditional education, that which is still received through human interaction rather than by electronic package, is becoming increasingly influenced by the new gatekeepers. Murdoch has financed a chair in communication studies at Oxford, and many universities offering degrees in media studies have sought part or full sponsorship from media companies who are not known to further the pursuit of truth or to protect the freedom of speech. The dangers of such sponsorship are well known. How likely is a course funded by Sky television to criticise that organisation? What message does a Murdoch chair of communications give to new generations of undergraduates?

> Information is power. The ability to make informed choices and delegate decision making to others distinguishes democratic society from anarchy. The freedom to express and communicate opinions distinguishes democratic societies from totalitarian regimes.

These were the opening words of a 1996 report from the Media and Communications Programme of the Institute for Public Policy Research (IPPR), an organisation set up by academic, business and trade union interests, to provide an alternative to the free-market think tanks.

Media policy on both national and international levels must address these issues if monopolistic or oligopolistic control over both the means and the content of digital communications are not to establish a power base that would challenge the very tenets of democracy. It is a concern which is echoed in the 1996 Media Manifesto of the Campaign for Freedom in Press and Broadcasting which calls for 'strong democratic accountability, quality and choice in the media' and by a joint policy statement by the two media unions – the Communications Workers Union (CWU) and the Broadcasting, Entertainment, Cinematograph and Theatre Union (BECTU) – which asserts that 'everyone must have easy and affordable access to broadband services to obtain employment, enjoy leisure, receive information, exercise citizenship and ensure democracy'.

Questions

A number of important questions are posed by the future development of TV broadcasting in the UK. What is the future of the BBC? Does the organisational split between broadcasting and production point to a time when the production base might be detached and privatised? Can the BBC maintain its claim to financing from the licence fee if the Corporation is increasingly dependent on commercial profits for its income? Will the Corporation continue to be controlled by a Board of Governors which is appointed by government? Can the governance of the BBC be reformed into something more democratic, open and accountable? Can the concept of public service survive in any form in either the ITV network or the BBC?

Will the ITV network be dominated by a small group of companies conceivably with large foreign participation? What effect will this have on programme policy? Will it lead to a decrease in local and regional programmes? Will it end up by discouraging 'difficult' and innovative programmes which advertisers see as a risk, as a threat to profitability? Will the growing influence of international financial interests in television lead to a homogenisation of programming, to the production of material that can be sold to broadcasting interests across the world and must therefore be part of that drive to global uniformity which is already present in fashion and in the market for pop music?

What will be the future of Channel 4? Will it be privatised because it has become profitable? Can it continue to be an innovative channel in the face of increasing commercial pressure? How successful will

Channel 5 be and what effect will its competition have on the ITV network and Channel 4?

Will the mass audiences that were once available be fragmented by niche television? Will television, as a result, cease to play its old social and cultural role?

Will access to the best of television come to depend on the ability to pay for programmes thus creating a two-tier viewing public?

Television does not have a high priority in the minds of politicians, whether they belong to the Labour Party, Liberal Democrat Party or Conservative Party, mainly because (apart from the size of the licence fee) the questions set out above are not thought to be of great political interest to the voters – although they are vital to them as viewers and citizens. There is however a critical debate going on in industry and education which is putting forward proposals for the future of the most important medium in our society. On a number of points there is agreement.

As far as the BBC is concerned the licence fee (famously described as the best bad way of funding the Corporation) should be maintained and linked to the retail price index (RPI). There is wide support for the view that appointments to the Board of Governors (of both the BBC and the ITC) should be made by a Select Committee of the House of Commons 'according to transparent criteria and procedures'. There are also calls for the abolition of the internal market – known as 'Producer Choice' – and for the BBC to continue in-house production at national and regional levels.

In the case of ITV, the main point of agreement is on the abolition of the auction for ITV licences and their allocation instead on the basis of the quality and viability of programming proposals. There should also be a commitment to regionally based programme production.

The coming of satellite television has raised worries about access. It has led to the suggestion that part of the spectrum should be reserved for universal service broadcasting, that is, a service for which no subscription is required. Satellite services should be required to carry a full range of public service programming.

As to who should be responsible for overseeing the converging services there is a proposal that the kind of rivalry that exists between the ITC and Oftel should be resolved by the appointment of a new overall regulator – OFCOM – who would be responsible for regulating both content and the delivery of programmes. The aim would be to achieve plurality and diversity in the media and the acceptance of USOs – universal service obligations – which require signals to be available to all and not merely to subscribers to a particular system. Above all there should be 'a continued emphasis on the political and cultural impact of broadcasting, and its implications for a democratic and pluralist society'.

The future shape of the television industry will be determined by political decisions taken at government level. These decisions will be determined by how that government perceives television – as an industry in which the market decides or as a medium which can provide a public service, supplying the Reithian trinity of information, education and entertainment. These are political issues that deserve to be addressed and discussed by viewers, by trade unions, by political party branches. A society – to coin a phrase – gets the kind of television it deserves.

Selected Reading

Briggs, Asa *The History of Broadcasting in the United Kingdom* (London: Oxford University Press, Vol. 1 1961, Vol. 2 1965, Vol. 3 1975, Vol. 4 1979, Vol. 5 1995). An official history relying heavily on BBC sources. Volume 4 deals with Competition (1955–1974).

Burns, Tom *The BBC: public institution and private world* (London: Macmillan, 1977). An important pioneering sociological account of the workings of the BBC.

Cathcart, Rex *The Most Contrary Region* (Belfast: The Blackstaff Press, 1984). An account by an ex-BBC executive of how the BBC 'coped with a profoundly divided society', Northern Ireland.

The Challenge of the Information Society (London: 1996). A joint policy statement by the Communications Workers Union and BECTU, the broadcasting and entertainment union, of the fundamental social issues raised by the convergence of the media.

Downing, John, Ali Mohannadi, and Annabelle Sreberny Mohammadi *Questioning the Media – A Critical Introduction* (London: Sage Publications, 1990). An excellent collection of essays on such topics as media, power and control, audiences and users, information technologies.

Cohen, Stanley and Jock Young (eds) *The manufacture of News: Social problems, deviance and the Mass Media* (London: Constable, 1973). An important discussion of the editorial processes behind newscasts.

Glasgow Media Group *Bad News* (London, Routledge and Kegan Paul, 1976) and *More Bad News* (London: Routledge and Kegan Paul, 1980). Critical examinations of the verbal and visual languages of newscasts.

Hill, Charles (Lord Hill) *Behind the Screen: the Broadcasting Memoirs of Lord Hill of Luton* (London: Sidgwick and Jackson, 1974). An account of British broadcasting by a politician who was chairman of the ITA and later of the BBC.

Hood, Stuart (ed.) *Behind the Screens, The Structure of British Television in the Nineties* (London: Lawrence & Wishart, 1994). A collection of critical essays by academics and practitioners on such topics as public service, ethnic programmes, independent production, etc.

Hood, Stuart and Garrett O'Leary *Questions of Broadcasting* (London: Methuen, 1990). A review of governmental broadcasting policy from the 1960s and an assessment of future developments based on interviews with those most closely involved.

Miller, David *Don't Mention the War* (London: Pluto Press, 1994). An account of how propaganda and (mis)information and news management has distorted reporting from Northern Ireland.

Murroni, Cristina, Richard Collins and Anna Coote (eds) *Converging Communications, Policies for the 21st Century* (London: Institute for Public Policy Research, 1996). A discussion of the problems of regulation in the age of cross-media ownership and digital broadcasting.

Report of the Committee on Financing the BBC (London: HMSO, 1986). The report of the Peacock Committee, setting out the market-based approach to broadcasting.

Shawcross, William *Murdoch* (London: Chatto & Windus, 1992). An authoritative biography of the media tycoon.

Stuart, Charles (ed.) *The Reith Diaries* (London: Collins, 1975). Fascinating material from the personal diaries of the founder of British broadcasting and the BBC.

Williams, Glanville *Britain's Media – How they are related* (London: Campaign for Freedom of Press and Broadcasting, 1994). A clear description of cross-ownership and the interlocking structures of the media industry.

Index